Marrying Later In Life

Elizabeth Berberich &
Marsha Connellan

Dearest Kelly:-
Wishing you a bright
future full of love
and adventure!
♡ Elizabeth ♡

For The Beautiful Brides of all Ages

To Our Husbands Stephen & Michael
*Who have made our lives the best they can be
capturing the true essence of what it is to love
and be loved*

&

Our Friends and Family
for their enthusiasm

Marrying Later in Life
Book Cover designed by
Savoir Faire Media
Printed in United States of America
ISBN-10: 9860134
ISBN-13: 978-9860134-0-9
Published by Hitched 4-A-Ride
California
www.marryinglaterinlife.com

If you are 40 years of age or older and getting married for the first time or tying the knot again, ***Marrying Later in Life*** is the book for you!

This is the BEST resource you should read before making any wedding decisions or plans. Start here, not with a wedding planner, to make your wedding day better than you ever dreamed it could be!

A growing number of marriages today are couples getting married later in life, and you may be among them. As an older bride, you will be facing challenges and issues that younger brides don't have to consider.

Concerns specific to mature brides include blending families, career and work decisions and legal issues, to name just a few.

Creating your own distinctive wedding style is also an essential. Choosing the right dress, it's accessories and planning will all be built around your style.

Find out the answers to these questions and much more in the extremely informative and interactive book, *Marrying Later in Life.*

Join Elizabeth and Marsha and learn how you too can be a "Beautiful Bride at Any Age!"

Table of Contents

About Our Book

About Our Book

Age does not protect you from love, but to some extent, protects you from age.
–Jeanne Moreau, actor, writer

"Marrying Later in Life" has been created just for you, a beautiful bride at any age. This book is a simple, uncomplicated guide for women, over the age of 40, who are getting married or remarried. It includes many important elements to help you create your perfect wedding as well as developing a solid foundation of communication, love and support in building a strong marriage. It is not meant to be a substitute for bridal magazines, wedding planners or the Internet, but a guide for answering the questions and concerns you might have when approaching the challenge of planning a wedding with the dynamics and issues associated with marrying later in life. Through our own experiences, and those experiences of other brides over the age of 40, we have produced an incredibly useful book: a book that is practical as well as functional and we hope will be extremely helpful in planning your wedding.

Our book is about the union of couples over 40 and the challenges they face when planning a wedding. Our personal journeys began several years ago when we finally met the men of our dreams and started to plan the perfect wedding. We both enjoyed the experience of arranging our "over 40" wedding ceremonies, but found we had many obstacles and unanswered questions along the way. How do you begin planning a wedding, your own wedding, not your son or daughter's? Where do you find a suitable dress? And then there is the most difficult issue – how do you combine your separate families in the ceremony so that everyone is happy? Looking for help in the bookstores and on the Internet was a futile endeavor and we could not identify another resource that addressed the issues we were encountering as we tried to plan our weddings.

"Marrying Later in Life" was written, first and foremost, as a resource for women who are planning a wedding but don't know where to begin. Throughout the book we share our experiences, as well as those of our friends, in the hope of assuring you that you are not alone during this joyful yet sometimes confusing time. Writing "Marrying Later in Life" has been fun. It has allowed us to take a break from our daily work commitments and to remember and savor the memories of our own weddings while helping others create their own special wedding celebration.

All of us have different stories about how we found the man we chose to marry. Throughout this book, we will endearingly refer to the man you have chosen to spend the rest of your life with as Mr. Wonderful. How you decide to celebrate your wedding day will depend on the man you have fallen in love with, your extended families, values, wishes and ideals.

∾∾

It is our hope that by reading "Marrying Later in Life" you will give yourself permission to make your wedding the one you have always imagined: the day you dreamed about when you were trying on your 6th bridesmaid dress and your mother said it was "very special" to be asked to participate in your second cousin's wedding; the day you wished for when you were the maid of honor for your little sister; the day you hoped for after you had been divorced for six months; the day when you were trying to understand how to re-enter the dating world; the day your ex-husband remarried. And now, all of that is behind you. It is your turn to be the bride and enjoy the day that will become one of the most memorable occasions of your life.

Always remember, there are customs, but no rules for "Marrying Later in Life." So, have fun creating the memories you both will cherish forever.

About Our Book Notes:

꙰꙰

CHAPTER ONE

YOU JUST SAID "YES"

What Comes Next?

AND QUIZZES

What Comes Next

"I dreamed of a wedding of elaborate elegance,
A church filled with family and friends.
I asked him what kind of a wedding he wished for,
he said one that would make me his wife."
– Author Unknown

Now that Mr. Wonderful has proposed and you are officially engaged to be married, it is time to discuss your wedding plans. These initial discussions are very important to you both, but especially you, the bride, since you will be the one in a position to make most of the decisions and carry out most of the details. However, the challenge of a bride, at any age, is to understand her groom's perception of his perfect wedding. His input is very important and must be interpreted and considered in reference to the style that you have envisioned, or may be developing, as you start the process of planning your wedding.

Most men have definite opinions but their ideas have not developed from months and years of daydreaming as yours have. So with this understanding, plan a special time to have a direct conversation in which you ask your fiancé about his vision of your wedding celebration. Try not to interject your opinions at this time; just take notes and ask questions if you want him to be more specific. Some men are uncomfortable about certain things and may not verbally express their opinions without being asked. The most important point at this time is to listen.

Your first conversation about the wedding may leave you with a lot of information, questions and concerns. This discussion will create some ideas that you will have to work with, or around, and it will also give your groom the confidence that you care about his opinions. Ask him if he has a vision of your wedding. Mr. Wonderful may not give you the answer you anticipated, but don't over react! You can develop the wedding of your dreams but you also need to be aware of your groom's ideas and suggestions as your wedding style evolves. Discuss as many of the details of your wedding as Mr. Wonderful wants to know or needs to understand. But don't neglect to discuss your specific plans just because you aren't sure you want his opinion. You know your groom, so you can anticipate the details you will need to discuss together as well as the details he will appreciate you taking care of without him.

To help Mr. Wonderful support you through the challenging process of planning a wedding, ask him what specific wedding details are important to him. Get him involved in picking out things he wants on the wedding registry and consider adding home electronics, power tools or camping gear to your list. Sometimes a group of friends will get together and want to buy you something different. Also, prepare your groom for the moments when you might experience "wedding overload" and need him to be there to make dinner or help you relax. Remind him that he is your buffer between family and friends who may get too enthusiastic and involved in their efforts to help with your wedding preparations. Tell him he is your best friend and that you depend on him to help you filter out petty worries from legitimate concerns.

While creating your wedding style, it is critical for you to feel comfortable and confident, but you need to be assured your groom is happy with your choices. This shouldn't be a problem because Mr. Wonderful chose you and your decisions are going to reflect the style of the person he loves. Sometimes your groom may simply want to have an opinion in order to feel involved and respected. To make sure he feels included, be prepared with two or three alternatives. You will most likely love one option more than the others, but make sure you can support them all with enthusiasm. You might be surprised at the benefits of offering Mr. Wonderful a choice. His opinions may help you with your own – or might reflect the blending of your styles.

Some engaged men might take a passive approach to their responsibilities regarding the wedding, unless they are educated early in the process. Planning a wedding is sometimes easier for the bride, who usually knows what she wants, but often isolates the groom. However, there are a lot of ways to make sure your fiancé is involved in the process of planning your wedding. We suggest you give him choices and encourage him to participate in areas that interest him. It is helpful and he will appreciate you giving him detailed directions for things you need him to take care of. Give Mr. Wonderful weekly and or monthly wedding-to-do lists so he can plan his wedding tasks on his own schedule and provide specific directions when you need his assistance if other tasks arise.

TIP: A good trade off is if you are in charge of all the wedding details, let him make the honeymoon plans!

Some Details for Mr. Wonderful to Manage

- What are his financial responsibilities for the wedding and honeymoon?
- What is his wedding attire going to be?
- Who are his groomsmen.
- What are the groomsmen's responsibilities?
- What are the groomsmen going to wear?
- What wedding venders is he responsible for?
- Are there any legal issues to be resolved?
- What are his financial goals?
- Has he made plans to get the wedding certificate?
- What are his fitness goals?
- Has he made his bridal registry requests?
- Does he want a bachelor party and where?
- Does he need dancing lessons?

Regardless of who takes on the different responsibilities of your wedding, always remember this will be one of the most memorable days of your life together. So have fun making it a celebration that reflects the love, hope and commitment you are asking your friends and family to witness and support.

What Comes Next Notes:

CHAPTER TWO

Big Decisions

AND QUIZZES

Big Decisions

Every romance has a story
Every union of two people comes with challenges

This chapter is the MOST IMPORTANT one you will read in our book. When a couple decides to get married, there are many important and difficult decisions that must be made. Some of the major decisions we want you to consider include blending families, work and career schedules, social and religious issues and where you are going to live. But the most difficult topic to discuss is finances which includes all of your assets and how you are going to manage them. Recognizing and having a comfortable conversation about the issues we address in this chapter might provide some new information about each other, help you make some choices, and hopefully help you identify the important things that need to be resolved before you get married.

You have finally found the man of your dreams, your soul mate for life. You are in a committed relationship and have decided to take the next step and get married. How do you imagine your life as a married couple? How does your fiancé imagine married life with you?

As a single woman, you have been living independently and making your own decisions for a long time. You have been able to support yourself, entertain yourself, give yourself a lot of attention and do the things you like to do without asking for anyone else's opinion. Now however, in this journey through life you have realized you don't want to start the day or end the day alone. You also want to share your daily experiences with someone special. You want to reach out and hold someone's hand affectionately whenever you feel the need. You want more than a best friend, a convenient lover or a companion. You are excited about including a special person in your life and you are confident your life will be fuller by sharing it with someone you truly love. Now, by some magical intervention, you have found the man you have been waiting for!

From the very beginning of your relationship, you must learn to discuss important matters together to make certain you and your fiancé understand each other's position. Remember emotion and attitude will influence one's perception, because what one person hears may not be what the other person said. If you feel any hesitation, unresolved questions or concerns, stop your wedding momentum until you both feel comfortable and have resolved your differences. Openly discuss the challenges you perceive evolving as you begin combining the important elements of your life. Marriage is not only a union of your souls but also a union of your resources and financial assets. Financial issues are one of three leading causes of marital friction and possibly the most critical. It is important for couples to talk openly and early in their committed relationship about questions or concerns that involve money in order to avoid any assumptions or misunderstandings down the road.

In the following chapters, we have created some quizzes to help you identify some choices you will have to make in the process of planning your wedding and getting married. These quizzes are designed to be fun, to open up lines of communication, and to help focus your attention on what we have identified as some of the big decisions you may have to make as a couple planning the rest of your life together. There are no right or wrong answers. Relax and have fun talking about things that may never have occurred to you. In the process, you may think of some we missed, so please email them to us at: info@marryinglaterinlife.com

How Well Do You Know Each Other Quiz

- What characteristics attracted you to your fiancé?
- Why did you decide to get married?
- How is your life going to change once you are married?
- What are your social reasons for getting married?
- What are your financial reasons for getting married?
- What will make you feel secure within the marriage?
- What daily routines are going to change once you are married?
- How do you describe the style in which you were raised by your parents?
- How were you disciplined?
- How were you rewarded?
- How would you describe your parent's marriage?
- What questions do you have about your fiancé's religious belief?
- How involved do you expect your fiancé to be with your family?

Previously Married Quiz for Couples

- What caused the breakup of your previous marriage?
- Looking back, what would you have done differently in your previous marriage?
- What type of relationship do you have with your previous spouse(s)?

CHILDREN

The secret to happy, later-in-life marriages often depends on the successful blending of their families. Today, over 65% of all marriages include children from previous relationships and this number is increasing.

Children are one of the most significant components to consider in the success of a new marriage. Everyone has to feel secure and included in your new family. With divergent personalities involved, this may not be possible at the outset. You are orchestrating the creation of a new family while maintaining the balance the family had before you got married.

It isn't that your children don't want to see you happy but they may fear losing some affection and a special part of you to someone else. Understand that this problem may manifest itself in many different ways, particularly in young children. However, the feeling is universal in all children who have to share their parent with someone new. Be flattered. Expect some uneasiness within a new household, discuss it and try to come to a smooth resolution before the wedding. Candidly discuss all the issues individually with each person involved and consider seeking an outside professional to help work through their fears and insecurities. There may be conflicts and challenges along the way but don't take them personally.

Your new situation will improve with time and tolerance on both sides. Don't let issues go unaddressed or ignore them in hope that they will get better with time. It is important you remain extremely sensitive to the feelings of everyone affected by your marriage. Communication, love and support are paramount during this time.

Anticipating and discussing some of the issues that can develop when combining families will make the transition smoother when the time comes for everyone to live together. Unless these issues are addressed in advance, you may not be prepared for the logistical complications and emotional stress that some new family members might bring to your home.

To this end, it is important for the children to participate in the wedding ceremony which will be a positive first step towards making them feel accepted, involved and part of a their new family. And hopefully, this will prevent them from reacting negatively towards the new spouse. If you are not their mother, our recommendation is do not try to be. Instead, be their friend; a person who is supportive, loving and encouraging in their daily lives.

A big decision is whether you and your fiancé want to have children together and it is a discussion you should have prior to getting married. Your decision to have more children may be significantly influenced by the number of dependents who are already a part of your new family and what your outstanding obligations are to them. You may be the primary caregiver for aging parents, your children may be older and getting ready to leave the home in a few years, or you may have logistical challenges with children from a prior marriage living between homes. There are a lot of complicating factors that can be affected by bringing another child into the family. Carefully evaluate your financial circumstances, your physical and emotional strength, and if the timing is right for your family to accept another sibling. Make sure your decision is mutual because it is a pivotal choice that could bring you more joy or create more challenges and tension in your everyday life as well as marriage. On the positive side, sharing the experience of having a child can solidify your marriage. The baby will represent the love and commitment between the two of you and may also be an emotionally necessary factor in securing and honoring the commitment you made to each other.

A significant consideration that you cannot disregard in having a child at this time of your life are the additional physical risks. Besides the physical health issues, there are also psychological considerations. If you have always yearned to have a child, having your own baby may be the most wonderful gift of your life but not always the wisest. If you are a mature bride, don't let your desire to have a child influence your decision to marry. Be honest with yourself and evaluate your motives, your circumstances and start your marriage with honesty. You may hope to have a child with Mr. Wonderful and this may be a deciding factor on whom you choose to marry and when. However, you don't have to be married to have a child or to obtain a child through adoption. If you are getting married because you want your own child, you are taking on a huge amount of emotional risk. Every mother will tell you raising a child is a full time job and it is not an easy way to start a marriage for either partner. Also, take into account, the age of your new child relevant to how old you will be when they are 13 or 18. Have you thought about the age difference between you and the parents of your children's friends? Will you be able to support and engage in their active growing up years which will include sporting and social activities? Carefully evaluate why you want a child, be confident it is a mutual decision and give yourself time to enjoy being newlyweds.

There are also many financial considerations if you want to add a child to your family, especially if you are supporting children from other relationships. Having another child opens up the question of who is going to care for the child in the home. If one of you decides to stay home, how will this decision affect each of your careers and your family income? You also have to prepare for the financial burden of your children's education at the same time you should be saving for your retirement. You may have forecasted your retirement about the time your child is ready for college!

If there is a significant age difference between you and Mr. Wonderful, it may not seem to be an issue at this time. However, you need to look 14 to 16 years into the future and recognize what your parenting responsibilities will be at that time. Don't ignore the issue if one partner wants more children and the other doesn't. Don't proceed with your wedding plans under the assumption that one of you will change your mind later on. This is an important matter and you must be comfortable with your decision about having or not having children before you go further into the relationship and start making wedding plans.

If you both think you would like to have children together, take time for your marriage to settle in and find its own balance. First, give yourselves time to enjoy the newness of your marriage and to develop normal daily routines and schedules. You both must feel secure in the marriage before you continue pursuing your dream of having more children.

Children and Other Dependents Quiz for Couples

- Do you want to have (more) children and why?
- If don't you want (more) children, why?
- If you are getting children with your marriage, how is this going to change your life?
- If you already have children, how is your marriage going to change their lives?
- What do you think your responsibilities should be for your fiancé's children?
- Are there any custody issues?
- What are your basic rules for disciplining your children?
- Excluding children, do you have any responsibilities for other members of your family?
- If you have responsibilities for someone other than yourself, what are they?
- How do you discipline your children?
- How do you reward your children?
- How should we tell our children we are getting married?
- Do you want your children to participate in the wedding, and if so, how do you want to include them?
- How long do you anticipate your children living with you?
- What major expenses do you anticipate your children will have before they leave home? (health insurance, dental care, education, wedding, etc.)
- Who is going to be responsible for these major expenses?

PETS

Combining families often includes bringing new pets into your home. Some people are attracted to unusual animals such as a potbelly pig or a snake, but the usual fare is either a cat, a dog, or multiples of each. So anticipate that you may be living with some new animals and prepare yourself for the challenges and joy these animals will bring to your home.

Some problems relating to having a pet may be pretty obvious, especially if someone is highly allergic to animal hair, a pet is aggressive around children, a family member is deathly afraid of an animal, or your fiancé just doesn't like your pet. You might have a problem because your pets don't get along with each other. Maybe one of your pets has not been well trained and gets on your furniture or has accidents on your carpet. You can't ignore these problems. Not everyone is an animal lover and pets can react like people to new situations.

Everyone loves their pet and it would not be a good beginning to your marriage if you expect your fiancé to give up something they love unless the situation was intolerable. Discuss the issues and evaluate how you are going to resolve them together. Be mindful of how you introduce the animals to their new home and to the people with whom they will be living. Ask your veterinarian for advice. If a child is afraid of an animal, try to understand why and work to eliminate those fears. If the pet does not have the manners you require for them to live in your home, take them to obedience classes. You can also assign special places in the house where the pet is allowed. But if the animal is dangerous, a mature decision has to be made not only for the safety of others living in the home but for your personal liability. It is important to acknowledge that some pet owners love their animals so much they are not aware of how others perceive them. So, broach the subject with tact and be prepared with positive solutions.

You may have tolerated each other's pets in the dating phase of your romance but now the reality of living with this animal does not make you happy. You may not like the pet because of some unpleasant experience you had with it. Animals are territorial and can get jealous. Or, you may be jealous of the pet! In a subtle way, the pet is taking attention away from you. Not everyone is an animal lover. Try to understand your fears and hopefully you will win the pet over and feel more comfortable with time. However, if you and Mr. Wonderful are at odds over this issue, you have to find a resolution. It isn't realistic to pretend the animal is not a problem and you don't want to find yourself plotting the pet's early demise.

Hopefully, you will find your pets are an integral component of your new family's personality and are considered an important part of your home. It may just be the dog or cat that brings the family together and helps create lasting memories.

Animal Quiz for Couples

- Do you like pets?
- What pets will you be bringing to the marriage?
- Are you co-parenting pets from a previous relationship?
- Do you want more pets?
- If so, what kind?
- If not, why?
- Do you have room for your combined family of pets?
- What do you think are your responsibilities for maintaining your pets?

∂∞∾

RELIGIOUS VALUES

Religious values are more structured and therefore easier to discuss. Religion is a personal belief system and it is more important to some people than others. While dating, you should have come to some understanding about the role of religion in each other's lives. If this is still an unresolved topic, don't put it off for another day. Religious, moral and family values are at the core of who we are and extend beyond the formality of attending weekly church services. If you have lingering religious concerns or differences, work toward resolving them before you commit to getting married. Stop the momentum and thoroughly discuss this issue. Many churches offer pre-marital counseling and personality tests for couples before they marry. These discussions often provide an interesting insight into the other's personality traits that aren't always obvious in the "honeymoon stage" of dating

---

Religious Quiz for Couples

- What is your religious background?
- If you are a Catholic and been married before, has your first marriage been annulled?
- Does it matter if we are of different faiths?
- Would you attend a church outside your religion?
- Does it matter to your family if you marry outside your faith?
- Do you attend church?
- How often do you attend church?
- What religious holidays do you observe?
- Do you have religious expectations of your finance?
- If so, what are they?
- If you have children, in what faith would you raise them?
- Is it important to be married in the church?
- Who would you like to have perform the wedding ceremony?
- Do you want to write your own vows?

SOCIAL VALUES

Social values are comprised of layers of subtle and undefined individual traits that, in a sense, dictate your way of life. They are acquired at an early age and are influenced by how you were raised. Raising a family, political matters, socialization, and how each of you approach and prioritize your daily activities all contribute to your individuality and they reflect your individual social values. In a short courtship, or when you haven't known someone for a long time, a person's values can often be hard to identify.

A person's morals and principles may not present themselves immediately in the early stages of a relationship. It is hard to adequately measure someone's values when you are so madly in love with them; they may not be apparent or even seem important to you if your attention is focused on romance. However, your fiancé's social values will dramatically impact your life and can become a critical issue later.

Successful long-term marriages have learned the importance of sharing the basic values of friendship and respect which are critical for maintaining a marriage. Having a good, solid relationship sounds simple to maintain, especially when you are in love with each other, but it takes a lot of work.

Remember, when life gets in the way, sustaining a strong marriage down the road can be challenging if you do not share the same basic values. Daily time management, merging schedules of children or elderly parents and financial matters are just a few of the things that will make your marriage more difficult if you do not understand each other's values and respect each other's differences.

Consider your marriage a "den of pleasure" and a "laboratory for growth".

21

Social Values Quiz for Couples

- What basic values were you raised with?
- What values do you like the most about your fiancé?
- What values do you share?
- What do you think are the most important values necessary for a happy, successful marriage?

MONEY MANAGEMENT

The most important way to avoid potential conflicts in the future is to be honest about your income and clearly define the areas of each person's financial responsibility from the very beginning of your marriage. We suggest you maintain several bank accounts to manage your combined financial resources. You need an account to pay your household, monthly bills and individual accounts for your discretionary expenses. This arrangement will allow you both some personal financial freedom. However, purchasing a new Harley-Davidson is another story!

One of your first financial discussion might be who is going to pay for the wedding? If this is your first marriage, your parents may have been waiting a long time to give you a wedding. But if that is not the case, deciding how you are going to pay for your wedding may be the first financial decision you make together. In our chapter, "Where to Spend the Dollars", you will find more information to help you make some of these wise and very important decisions.

Money Management Quiz for Couples

- Do you want to create a family budget?
- How many bank accounts do you want to establish?
- Who will pay the household expenses and manage the checkbook?
- Which bills will be considered household expenses?
- Which bills will be considered personal?
- What percent of your income do want to allocate to savings and investments?
- What percent of your income do you want to allocate to your personal accounts?
- When making financial decisions, how much can each of you spend without consulting the other?
- Who is going to manage savings and investments?
- How will your financial arrangement be affected if one of you is working and the other is retired or has never worked?
- What are your financial priorities?
- If children are involved, how will they be provided for and by whom?

❧

LIVING ARRANGEMENTS

Living together is a big step in a relationship and many couples decide to make a home together before they marry. Whether you start living together before you marry or after your wedding, there are a lot of decisions to be made that may not be limited to what the two of you want. Beginning a new marriage with just you and Mr. Wonderful is ideal but not always a reality. You not only have to decide where you want to live but your discussion should also include who else will be affected by your decision. Between you and Mr. W, you may have multiple residences in different parts of town or in different states. You may have children going to different schools. You might have elderly parents that now depend on your care. You must look at all the variables when deciding where you are going to combine your households. Itemize all the decisions you have to make and prioritize what is important to you individually. This will prepare you for the compromises that might be necessary in the process of resolving all your issues.

Getting married is so much more complicated than combining two house-holds of furniture.

Living Arrangements Quiz for Couples

- Where do you want to live?
- What issues affect your decision of where to live?
- How will your life change if you have to move?
- Who do you think will be living with you after your marriage?

❧

SOCIAL AND OUTSIDE INTERESTS

Each of you has developed a lifestyle of your own while you were single. Mr. Wonderful's way of life, routines and standard of living may have appeared exciting and new while you were getting to know each other. However, over time and with the commitment of marriage some of your differences may begin to cause friction. It's best to recognize your differences now and make a plan on how to resolve them. Remember marriage is a compromise and you must learn to establish a balance and respect each other. If each of you has come from different backgrounds and interests, acknowledge these differences and talk about how you might combine some of them into shared activities.

You may also be bringing together two different energy levels, social skills, habits, multiple interests and friends. You may not enjoy some activities equally and you may have different sleeping schedules. Some people need to sleep, or like to sleep, more than others and some of us just enjoy "more quiet time." Respect each other's "alone time" and don't feel threatened or insecure because of it. Some of these issues may have been apparent while dating, but most were overlooked as your relationship evolved and your time was spent almost exclusively with each other. It is important to identify the social and outside interests you enjoy doing together and the things you would rather continue doing alone or with other friends. You will be together for the rest of your life and you need to maintain your individuality as well as establishing your personality as a couple.

Social and Outside Interest Quiz for Couples

- When you are not working, what is your favorite thing(s) to do?
- What social activities and outside interests are important to you?
- What social activities and outside interests do you want to do together?
- What social activities and outside interests do you want to do by yourself?
- What social activities and outside interests do you want to do with other friends?
- What activity level are you comfortable with?
- How do you like to entertain?
- Who do you like to entertain?
- Where do you like to travel?
- How do you like to travel?
- What do you like to do for relaxation?
- What do you like to do for excitement?
- What are your favorite things to do?
- What don't you like to do?

WORK AND CAREER DECISIONS

It is important for each partner to clearly understand and support the other's career and personal goals on a daily, weekly and yearly basis. Each partner needs to know the time and emotional obligations the other needs to fulfill their commitments. How each of you manage and support these differences will directly affect you and your marriage. This is especially important if either of you have a job that requires a lot of travel, work unusual hours, own your own business, work from home, or if one of you has a job and one of you doesn't. Your decisions may be based on many different circumstances. But if you have choices, the decision for one of you to stay home should be mutually understood. It is just as important to recognize the value of the person staying home as it is the person bringing home the paycheck.

Depending on your ages, one or both of you may have been retired when you met and your goals at that point of your lives were completely different. This will present some challenges, especially if the one who has retired wants a daily companion. If your husband retires first, and he is pressuring you to join him in retirement, help him understand what your job means to you. His career may not have been as satisfying as yours or he may have had to retire for health reasons. Don't quit working until you are ready and remind Mr. Wonderful you have married him for better or worse - but not for lunch.

When marrying someone who is going to retire or has retired, discuss what expectations they have for who performs the daily routines and chores. Also, talk about how much time you each want to spend together and how much time you want to devote to your own activities. As a couple, it is important to have some common interests that you can enjoy together but being together 24/7 isn't always the best situation. Coming together at the end of the day, and sharing what you did or accomplished when you were apart, will add another dimension to your relationship and give you more to talk about.

> ## *Work and Career Decisions Quiz for Couples*
>
> - In what areas are you qualified to get a job?
> - If you had a choice, what job would you like to have? If you could not find a job, how would you earn some money?
> - What would change if you did not have a job?
> - When do you plan on retiring?
> - If you stopped working, how would your life change?
> - Who will manage the household and how will the chores be allocated?
> - How do you see your career in ten, twenty and thirty years from now?
> - What are your goals in ten, twenty or thirty years?
> - What short-term goals will you need to accomplish to achieve your objectives?
> - What long-term term goals will you need to accomplish to achieve your objectives?
> - What are your goals as a couple in ten, twenty or thirty years?

MAINTAINING OR CHANGING YOUR NAME

When you marry, taking your husband's last name is traditional and it identifies to whom you are married. However, you do have some alternatives if you don't want to drop the surname you were using before you got married. In some situations it is easier to keep your name as it is or use both surnames. The popular consensus is to use a hyphen between your present last name and your husband's surname which will keep you under your current name alphabetically but identify you as having a changed or new status. However, this can also create some confusion. There are situations that do not recognize hyphenated names and they either combine the names, or as the government does on passports, use your first surname name as your middle name. This requires you to carry a second form of ID to clarify why the name on your airline reservation is not exactly as it reads on your passport. In summary, you will experience complications with any decision you make. You just have to decide what name you want to be recognized under. This may depend on your age, your career, your visibility in the community, which name is easier to say and spell and how your husband feels about it. It's important to talk this over with Mr. Wonderful to confirm he does not have a strong opinion one way or the other. In the event he has an opinion about what name you use, try to understand why it is an issue with him and see if you can come to a compromise. You might solve the problem by using your previous name for business and your new married name socially.

Changing your name is not a trivial issue. Remember, you are the one who will have to manage the confusion created by taking on a completely new name at this time of your life. If you have children, it will mean you won't have the same last name. Changing your name involves changing your driver's license, passport, credit cards, health records, social security information, previous legal and financial documents, as well as anything else under which you are identified by your birth or previous surname.

Whatever you decide, make the transition slowly and when and where it is appropriate. If you have a business or professional identity, we suggest you continue to be acknowledged under the name you are identified with in those circumstances, especially if your career has spanned many years or decades. With time, it will be easier to assume your new married name if that is what you choose.

Maintaining or Changing Your Name for Couples Quiz

- What do you have to consider before deciding to change your name?
- How will changing your name impact your life both personally and professionally?
- Under what name do you want to be identified after your wedding?
- What will you have to do if you change your name?

PRENUPTIAL AGREEMENT

A prenuptial agreement is a written contract between two people, who are about to marry, which outlines the terms of possession of assets, treatment of future earnings, control of the property of each, and potential division if the marriage is later dissolved. These agreements are fairly common if either or both parties have substantial assets, children from a prior marriage, inheritances, high incomes, or have been "taken" by a prior spouse. The prenuptial is an agreement that is a binding legal document signed prior to the wedding date. It spells out which assets will be marital and shared, and which will remain separate in case of a divorce or death.

One of the most sensitive but extremely important issues couples face when marrying later in life is the discussion of financial resources. Obviously you have been successful at dating. You are now engaged. Your family and friends are all excited. If you have children, they have accepted the reality of having a new parent, which is a huge concept for any child at any age. You have resolved your combined living arrangements and have reached a decision for both of your career paths. When you are comfortable with all of these issues, it is a good time to put your decisions in writing in the form of a prenuptial agreement.

We are going to call the prenuptial agreement a "Prenup" which seems to be a friendlier term to take away the concern and anxiety created by the process. Talking about these issues up front may feel like you are planning your divorce before the wedding and it can become a very emotionally charged discussion. No one wants to think about the possibility of your marriage ending, especially when you are planning your wedding and your future which should be one of the most joyous time of your life! Our advice is to create your prenuptial early. Be prepared for an emotional reaction within yourself, or from your groom, but try to work through it rationally. Remember, you are working with a legal issue and a specific structure that has to be followed. Both parties need separate representation for the prenuptial to be legally valid and we do not recommend trying to prepare it on the Internet.

Don't forget you are a modern mature bride entering this legal union with your previous life as part of who you have become. You have achieved a lot as well as accumulated a significant amount of financial assets, and it is important to protect your accomplishments. Define what you will be happy and eager to have identified as community property inside the marriage and be clear what assets will remain your individual, personal property. Discussing the division of your assets is not romantic but it is necessary in planning for a successful marriage.

You are in love, you are very happy and you don't want anything to spoil the glow but you have to deal with the reality of the situation. The challenge is making sure everyone wants the same thing. If this is not the case, then you must decide on a financial compromise for your future together. Remember, what you think you said, may not be what the other person heard. Unless these issues are discussed and clarified, it is the most significant grounds for disagreement later on that may lead to a future divorce. If you want to avoid bringing up this uncomfortable subject, have a trusted financial consultant such as your attorney, accountant or financial planner raise the issue. If you need a third party to negotiate the basic issues of your financial union, you need to recognize the pattern you are setting for dealing with difficult issues within your marriage.

Assets and liabilities need to be recognized and appropriately dealt with at the beginning. Some decisions may be too important or legally confusing for you to make on your own, so legal counsel is critical to producing an appropriate document. This is an extremely important part of your relationship and you need to be knowledgeable, involved, and part of the decision process. It is a difficult but extremely important document to work through and accomplish, but it will help to eliminate any questions and uncomfortable moments down the road. A strong bond of trust will begin with full disclosure of each other's debts and assets. Don't let the magic and happiness of your engagement take away your responsibility to make independent decisions about the assets you have acquired prior to your marriage.

Having this conversation and acting on these decisions is critically important to understanding what your marriage is going to mean to each other financially. In your discussions, it is important to understand that the "Prenup" is a document that can be changed in a postnuptial addendum or in your living trust or will. The prenuptial is where you are financially starting your marriage. It is far better to be clear on financial issues at the start and resolve any conflicts and misunderstandings before progressing further with your wedding plans. Money can be a source of insecurity and concern, whether you are the one who has it or the one who doesn't. This goes for all partnerships. Marriage just amplifies the issue because there are so many emotions involved.

As you get older, your personal worth will most likely increase substantially over your lifetime. Your assets may include earning potential, a family business, property, financial investments or anything else of monetary value. What can or will become community property once you are married needs to be clarified and understood according to your state laws. Each state has different parameters and regulations pertaining to tax, divorce and inheritance issues. This is another good reason for you to consult a lawyer in order to prepare a proper document that exclusively represents your personal decisions.

Inheritance is a tough discussion especially when there are children from previous marriages. A trust is a good way to protect assets for your children when you die. And if needed, still allows your partner to draw an income from the interest earned from the trust for the remainder of his life. The principle would then pass to your children upon your husband's death. Wills and trusts are discussed in more detail later in this chapter.

Another financial concern when marrying later in life is one's health. If one of you is much older than the other, provisions must be made for your partner's healthcare in case of an emergency or entering a nursing home because of an illness. In most states, spouses are responsible for each other's medical bills, including bills for long-term health care. Unless one of you has had the experience of losing a loved one to a long, debilitating illness, this problem has probably never been an issue either of you have thought to discuss. Especially at the beginning of your new life together - but you should. Buying long-term health insurance before you walk down the aisle will prevent you both from wiping out your savings in the event of an illness.

Look at the bright side, creating a "Prenup" is an opportunity to have an open and honest discussion about financial issues that could become potential time bombs later in your marriage. Making these decisions before the ceremony will add to the health and longevity of your relationship. It will also help make the existing children of both families more comfortable and accepting of your new lives together. Family members just want to be happy. No one wants to feel threatened either emotionally or financially by your decision to marry.

Be brave! One partner may feel very adamant while the other may feel threatened by defining financial differences. However, do what you think is in your best interest and the best interest of those in your extended family. If your significant other gets upset, try to put yourself in their emotional position and be sensitive to his concerns. However, don't back down if you think something is the best decision for your interests. If a prenuptial becomes a major obstacle in your wedding harmony, communicate about what the problems are and work through them. This is where the strength of your marriage partnership of open and honest discussions will begin. Don't minimize these issues if you have concerns or there is conflict. This is a very tough process. If you can't get through a financial discussion now, then how are you going to address other difficult issues as they come up in your marriage?

Prenuptial Quiz for Couples

- How do you feel about preparing a prenuptial agreement?
- What do you want to include in your prenuptial agreement?
- What are your assets and what are your outstanding debts?
- What do you want to know about your finance's assets and outstanding debts?
- What are your financial goals for the future?
- What do you have to do to achieve your financial goals?
- What type of insurance do you think you both need?
- How do you want to manage your tax situation?
- Who do you look to for financial and legal advice?

ॐॐ

POSTNUPTIAL AGREEMENT

As with the prenuptial, post-nuptials are used to decide the division of assets and income with death or divorce. It will protect past assets, clarify the division of future assets and identify who would be responsible for managing the debts and assets created during the marriage. Postnuptial agreements can also include inheritance or business issues, limit the future number of children in the marriage, how one partner will care for the other if fallen ill, decide who gets the animals in the event of divorce and even who gets buried where!

The most important reason for a pre or postnuptial agreement is to reduce marital strain by setting forth expectations and obligations in your marriage. If there are circumstances that preclude you from having a "Prenup", you can still prepare a postnuptial agreement. However, each of you may have lost the opportunity or ability to negotiate because the terms of the document may be constricted by the fact you are already married. There are certain state laws that immediately affect the rights of each partner once married. In this case, one partner may not want to amend the marriage contract.

Postnuptial Quiz for Couples

- Why do you want a postnuptial agreement if you did not want a prenuptial agreement?

❧

WILLS AND TRUSTS

Wills and trusts are two main documents for protecting your assets and providing for your loved ones after your death. It is important to understand the difference between the two and how they can be beneficial to you and your estate.

A will is a legal document that allows you to specify who will inherit your property after you die and identifies a guardian for your child if they are under age. Without a will, you will have no say in what happens to your property. Even if you create a will, it is important to understand that your estate will still go through probate.

Probate is the legal process that an estate passes through to make sure your property is distributed in accordance with your will or according to the laws of the state if there is no will. The probate process usually takes about a year to be completed, as the validity of the will must be established. Those who have a vested interest in your property, as well as all your heirs and creditors, must be alerted of your death and any disputes over the will must be resolved in probate court. However, you can save your heirs from the process of probate if you have established a trust.

A trust is a separate legal entity from your will to protect your property and assets from probate, taxes and public scrutiny. Trusts may be established while you are living or upon your death as set forth in your will. There are many types of trusts to choose from, and the type you establish will determine how much control you have over the property that you will place within the trust. Contact a reputable attorney if you need help establishing a trust or creating a will that will not be deemed invalid or delay the disbursement of your property.

You will probably have to draw up a new will or trust after you marry or remarry. This new document must include the details of your pre or postnuptial agreement, who has been designated as the power of attorney, your beneficiary designations, IRA plans, bank accounts, life insurance policies, health directives and other portfolio investments.

Wills and Trust Quiz for Couples

- What is the difference between a Will and a Trust?
- What legal documents do you already have in place?
- How will you change your Will or Trust after you marry?
- What assets will you allocate to your husband and what assets will be left to your children, family members, valued friends and/or charities?

WEDDING INSURANCE

Wedding insurance protects a couple from circumstances beyond their control. The average cost of most weddings today is $25,000-$50,000 and it is an investment that needs to be protected from unforeseen disasters. From the planning stage to the day of the wedding, there are many things that can happen to postpone or disrupt your event.

Wedding insurance carriers offer a variety of products covering different financial risks involved in planning a wedding. For instance, these could include inclement weather, airline cancellations, illness or some other unexpected event. This would be especially important to look into if you are having a destination wedding.

The most common policies include expenses for transportation, the wedding dress, catering, wedding rings, flowers and photography. As with any financial decision, comparing wedding insurance coverage is a prudent thing to do. What you want to insure depends on your priorities and on the amount that you have invested in each area.

The best wedding insurance is the one that you can afford and fits your budget. That is why you must evaluate the different insurance packages covering the events and items most important to you. Take note that the best wedding insurance is not chosen merely based on price. In today's world, you want to buy a policy from an agent who represents a company that is not going to go out of business. So the cheapest wedding insurance is not necessarily the best. Obviously, the best wedding insurance is the one that offers the most coverage for the most affordable price from the most reputable company.

As with buying any insurance, you have to choose a wedding insurance provider that you can trust. The logical place to start is with the insurance agent you are currently working with for your other insurance coverage. If your agent does not represent a company that offers wedding insurance, ask your wedding consultant, or friends who have recently had a large wedding, for their recommendation. The Internet is probably the best resource for comparing insurance policies. Most reputable providers

All of these personal discoveries and emotions are great and very real but there are many more things to be considered before being married…and some very big decisions that have to be made.

post the terms and conditions on their websites. With this information, you will be able to decide whether a certain insurance company provides the right insurance for your needs. Ask for references, read the small print or take it to your lawyer before signing and paying for the policy.

Of course you want to the find the most complete package for the least amount of money which may be accomplished with a customized policy. Some companies offer an on-line program where you can create your own policy and the website will immediately provide you with a calculation of your premium. Some Internet sites even offer discounts.

As with most decisions, you must take your time to find the best wedding insurance. While it will take additional funds to purchase the insurance, it's an investment you hope you won't have to use. However, it is worth your peace of mind as well as your pocketbook.

The Bridal Association of America will also have information on carriers who have expertise in this area.

Wedding Insurance Quiz for Couples

- What could happen if you do not have wedding insurance?
- Where would you look for wedding insurance?
- What elements of your wedding are important or worth the expense to be insured?

❧

MARRIAGE CERTIFICATE

A Marriage certificate is a legal document stating that an Officiate has married you under the laws of that particular state and that the ceremony has been witnessed by two individuals. It is a binding legal record that authenticates the marriage and the ceremony cannot be performed without it.

The marriage certificate has to be obtained in the state in which you are getting married. The rules may change slightly from state to state but we have provided the guidelines for California since that is the state in which we reside. The regulations may be slightly different for other states. But in all states, the Officiate can not perform a legal ceremony without a marriage certificate.

Many county clerks perform civil marriage ceremonies in their offices. If you need more information regarding civil marriage ceremonies in your state/county, contact your county clerk's office directly to see if they provide this service.

As an example, the rules for obtaining a marriage license in the state of California are:

- You do not need to be a California resident to marry in California.
- To marry in California, both parties may not be already married to each other or other individuals!
- The marriage Officiate and the witnesses must be physically present when the marriage is performed.
- Blood tests are NOT required to obtain a marriage license.
- Both parties must appear in person and bring a valid picture identification to the County Clerk's Office to apply for a marriage license. Valid picture identification is one that contains a photograph, date of birth, and an issue and expiration date such as a state issued identification card, drivers license, passport, military identification, etc. Some counties may also require a copy of your birth certificate.
- If you have been married before, you will need to know the specific date your last marriage ended and how it ended (Death, Dissolution, Divorce or Nullity). Some counties may require a copy of the final judgment if your previous marriage ended by dissolution.

- Marriage licenses are valid for 90 days from the date of issuance.

California Family Code states the persons who are authorized to solemnize marriage ceremonies in California are:

- A priest, minister, or rabbi of any religious denomination
- A judge or retired judge
- A magistrates or retired magistrate
- A legislator, constitutional officer of the state or a member of Congress
- Or your best friend who has completed an online application to be an Officiate of the Universal Church of Life

The person solemnizing the marriage must return the original marriage license to the County Clerk or County Recorder within 10 days of the date of the ceremony. The fees and costs applying to the license will vary depending on your location.

Don't forget this very important document and plan ahead especially if you are having a destination wedding. Marsha's daughter was caught up with the last minute details of her destination wedding and thought she could simply run into the local courthouse and pick up an application for the certificate. She was quite shocked when the clerk told her she needed the groom to be present. The marriage certificate isn't something you can take home, sign and send back in the mail!

If marrying abroad, you may have to arrange for a civil ceremony at your local courthouse before you leave the country to make sure your marriage is legitimate in the United States. This information can be found on the Internet or you can check with your local government office to understand the procedures you will need to follow.

If you get married out of the country, make sure you have thoroughly researched the marriage laws for that country. You may also find the American Consulate helpful in providing specific knowledge you should have prior to planning a wedding in a foreign location. Also, when making your flight arrangements be sure to book your flight in the same name as your passport. Many brides have been left crying on the other side of the security gate because, in their excitement, they booked their flight under their new, married name.

Marriage Certificate Quiz for Couples

- Where do you want to get married?
- What are the laws for getting married in that location, i.e. marriage certificate?
- Who do you want to be your Officiate and witnesses?

འ❦ཤ

All of these personal discoveries and emotions are great and very real but there are a lot more to be considered before being married…and some very big decisions that have to be made.

Big Decisions Notes:

∂∾∾

CHAPTER THREE

Style

AND HOW YOU DETERMINE YOURS

AND QUIZZES

Style

*"Why change? Everyone has his own style. When you have found it you
should stick to it."*
-Audrey Hepburn

We constantly reference the word "style" throughout our book because it is a word that describes how you interpret your world and differentiates you from everyone else. We have chosen to elaborate on this word because we want you to recognize and focus on your style as you make decisions about your wedding. Your unique style will be reflected in every decision you make from the invitations you choose to accessories you decide for your wedding dress. Someone's style is hard to identify and describe in words because it is a personal characteristic combining many elements and everyone is different. As we mature, our style may change or adjust to accommodate different factors or situations but it will always reflect our uniqueness. Your wedding will also be making a style statement about you and Mr. Wonderful because it will reflect your style as a couple.

WHAT IS STYLE?

Style is a specific or characteristic manner of expression. It reflects your originality and makes you distinctively unique. Some words that describe ones style are inner quality, flair, polish, grace, sophistication, spirit, charm, mood and mannerisms.

Your personal style is influenced by your attitude which can be sparkling, distinctive, clear, commanding, friendly, polished, brilliant, conventional, captivating, simple, flamboyant, soft, engaging, dramatic, elegant, ambitious, poetic or dazzling.

The type of clothes you select also identifies your style. Clothing choices can be tailored and classic, frilly and floral, sleek and professional, balanced and concise, pleasing and correct, showy or conservative, impeccable or authentic and many more combinations.

As you develop and mature, you begin to establish your own unique style. Parents, siblings, friends and your environment influence how you see yourself. Your basic character comes from within and is how you have learned to define yourself, what you like, don't like and what makes you feel good!

Your personal style can be expressed in countless ways and can apply to many objects and possessions as well as the way you relate to others. Style is not limited to fashion or the latest trend. It is not determined by the expense of a particular item but instead by the "look", color and design. Your style is an innate part of who you are which is determined by your personal preferences and the way you present yourself to the world. Your family background plays a role but your personal style is a part of who you have developed into as a person through the years. It is one's "life" style. It shows your originality and makes you distinctive. Style is an internal understanding of what you like and makes you comfortable and happy. You reflect your style in all the choices you make.

Your distinctive style is reflected in everything you have chosen to surround yourself with in your home and throughout your daily life. It is everything you buy, including the color you paint your kitchen, the car you drive, the flowers you plant, what your favorite chair looks like, what you like to wear when no one will see you, as well as how you wear your hair when you want to look special.

As you have grown into your personal style, you have learned, sometimes painfully, what looks best on you. Your style does not fit into any one category but is a combination of several things that have impressed you and affected the way you perceive the world. It is how you visually express yourself which over time you have molded into your very own unique look.

You know which colors and styles you are comfortable wearing. You choose styles you know look best on your figure and you have learned how to adapt the most current fashions and make them uniquely yours. You understand how to accentuate and compliment your best features and have learned to stay away from styles that bring attention to areas of your body that have changed when you weren't looking! As a modern mature woman, you know how to camouflage your less attractive features and buy clothes that focus on your best qualities.

Paying attention to your personal style will help you keep in touch with how you look to others, give you self-confidence and help direct your shopping so you choose clothes that differentiate and compliment your uniqueness.

When planning your wedding, your personal tastes will be reflected in every aspect of your event. The most wonderful thing about getting married at this time of your life is you can create a wedding of your wildest dreams without following traditional protocol found in wedding manuals. Don't be afraid to create your own unique wedding style. The limitations are only within you, your budget and the people with whom you want to share this intimate moment. From the very first decision you make, to the final touches, your wedding will describe who you are and the joy you feel being in love.

YOUR WEDDING STYLE

As a couple, you and Mr. Wonderful have decided to marry which means you are both bringing together different styles or a different perception and interpretation of the same thing. You know you have the same sense of style at some level or you wouldn't have been attracted to each other. You may have merged some of your style concepts as you have developed as a couple but now you will be applying them to your wedding which will take some thought and communication. If you and Mr. Wonderful have some disagreements along the way, you will learn how to come to some compromise. However, if you can't make wedding decisions together, step back from the situation and try to evaluate why.

Is one of you just being stubborn and insensitive or is there a power play going on?

If you can't make the relatively easy decisions about the details of your wedding, this may reflect the way you will interact in your marriage when some decisions are more important. At some level, you clearly have the same sense of style or you wouldn't have been able to form the bond that has led you down your path to marriage. Be brave, be open and be positive because once you start making some of the initial wedding decisions together, the rest of the details will fall into place.

We suggest you start your wedding plans by deciding on your location. Begin with generalities such as a ceremony on the beach or in the local church. If you find your discussion is going off in different directions, each of you must make a list prioritizing a specific number of places you would like to get married. From your lists, hopefully there will be several similar choices. Your location may limit your options for the date, but once that is determined, you can start a timeline for the rest of your decisions.

Defining your style at the beginning is imperative. Start by getting a firm grasp on the specific look you want to create from your invitations down to the ceremony and reception. This pivotal decision will influence the rest of your wedding style choices. It may be overwhelming at first but once you are focused your decisions will be easier. You won't be constantly second guessing yourself, changing your mind and correcting mistakes. All of which wastes time, money and energy.

When deciding on your wedding style, don't be intimidated by the image of youth and the ideas magazines and media portray as the perfect bride. Celebrate and be positive about who you are and what you look like today. This doesn't mean that you aren't the image of beauty and elegance but remember you aren't 21 anymore. Then again, do you really want to be 21? Respect and enjoy your age and the woman you have become because you are unique!

HOW DO YOU DETERMINE YOUR WEDDING STYLE?

There are three basic wedding formats when creating your wedding style: formal, semi-formal or casual. The style you choose will dictate all your wedding choices from your dress to the final moments of the day.

This is the beginning of creating your style together as a couple. Mr. Wonderful is the man you have been waiting to find all of your life. You love and respect him and consider his opinions valid and important. All of which you must remember as you discuss the details of the wedding you will be planning together.

As the bride, it is your wedding day but it is important you understand how much Mr. Wonderful wants to be involved or how much you expect him to contribute to the details of planning the wedding. Mr. Wonderful will be supportive of your ideas and decisions because he loves you, wants you to have the wedding of your dreams and may not really care about the specific details involved in getting married. He just wants to be married.

It is important to evaluate and understand each of your own personal styles. If they are very different, consider how you are going to incorporate his ideas in the process of making your decisions. It is important not to take it personally if Mr. Wonderful has his own opinions. He may feel like he is being supportive and involved by adding a suggestion or two which may also give you additional insight into his style.

Remember that men love to be the problem solvers. Make him feel comfortable by creating an open discussion in which he can express his ideas and not just contribute what he thinks you want to hear. To organize yourself to discuss different options and to incorporate Mr. Wonderful's suggestions, it is important to be prepared with alternatives to the choices you present to him. You will probably love one style more than the other but be sure you can support both with equal enthusiasm. He cares deeply about you and wants to please you especially at this time. Consider yourself fortunate to have a groom that is interested in the wedding details and wants to be included. These opportunities to make choices together will build a pattern of how you will make decisions as husband and wife in the future.

Your style will be reflected in every aspect of your wedding: where and when the ceremony will take place, your stationery, the invitations, your dress and accessories. From the first decision that you make to the final touches, your wedding will express the importance of this day and will reflect the joy you both feel being in love.

Style Quiz for Couples

- What is your definition of style?
- What words would you use to describe your style?
- What words would you use to describe your fiancé's style?
- How are your styles the same?
- How are your styles different?
- What wedding styles do you like?

From the following list, prioritize, from most to least, the wedding elements you think are most important. At this point don't concern yourself with $$$.

- Wedding Ceremony
- Dress, Accessories
- Location
- Reception
- Atmosphere, Decor
- Size of wedding
- Flowers
- Music
- Stationery
- Caterers

- Table Favors
- Liquor
- Wedding Consultant
- Officiate
- Photographer
- Rehearsal Dinner
- Hair and Make-up
- Rehearsal Dinner
- Wedding Breakfast
- Honeymoon
- Website

DEVELOPING YOUR STYLE AS A BRIDE

The time has finally arrived to walk down the aisle with the one you have chosen to love, honor and cherish for the rest of your life. When your wedding date has been set and the location is determined, "The Dress" is the next most important decision you will make because the style you choose will be reflected in your other wedding decisions. We have prioritized determining the location of your event above choosing your dress because selecting something suitable for a wedding on the beach is much different than choosing a dress for an elegant, church wedding. However, if what you are going to wear on your wedding day has already been determined before selecting your wedding venue, you will have to make the rest of your wedding plans work around this decision.

It is important to consider how Mr. Wonderful likes you to dress. Always keep in mind his preferences and don't neglect his favorite looks and styles. He is the one for whom you want to create a lasting impression. Does he prefer old fashioned and frilly or sleek and sexy? Would he prefer a more traditional conservative look or does he like you to wear trendy clothes? It is important to remember that he is the one you are walking down the aisle toward and you will both always enjoy reminiscing about this moment for the rest of your lives.

We found the first challenge in finding the perfect dress, or wedding outfit, is getting started and starting early! Whether you buy your dress at a bridal salon or a designer showroom, it is important to understand they have to follow a specific timeline when ordering your dress. It can take from six weeks to six months from the day you order your dress to your final fitting! Therefore, if you have time it is ideal to start looking for your wedding dress nine months before your wedding date. This will give you time to find your dress and accommodate the six months it usually takes to order, receive, and if necessary, alter your dress.

There are a lot of big and little details that accompany the selection of your wedding gown and you will need to recognize these before you start to look for your dress and purchase it. You must absolutely love the gown you choose or you should keep looking. It is a big decision and a major expense so be certain it is the perfect dress for you. Understand that you probably can't take the dress back as you might be able to do with the purchase of any other dress.

If you can't get interested in looking for your gown, you should evaluate your feelings about moving forward with the wedding. Your hesitation may be interpreted in many ways. You may not want to commit to the expense of a wedding dress, maybe you don't really want to have a large, public wedding, or maybe you do not feel ready to get married. Your reluctance to commit to a dress may be an indication of some deeper issues and you should have a talk with yourself and then with Mr. Wonderful.

Some women have always dreamed of wearing a certain style wedding dress, but if you don't have a particular style in mind, try to formulate a mental picture of how you want to look on your wedding day. The way you envision yourself will help you to develop a dress concept. To get started, build a picture file of dresses or outfits that appeal to you the most.

You will be amazed at the number of bridal magazines available. They have become specialized by geographical area, season and projected cost of the wedding. Go through as many of these magazines as you have the time and interest. Tear out anything that appeals to you. Pay attention not only to the dress but also to the hairstyles, shoes, flowers and any other accessories and accents you find interesting because you may want to refer to them later. Starting with the dress, line up all of the pictures on the floor and rate them in the order of your favorites to see if there are similarities in design, color and length.

The Internet is a great resource but it is helpful to have a few specifics in mind so you can limit your search. If you search by "bridal dress" you will be overwhelmed with the number of sites that are available. But if you have a general idea of what you are looking for such as a bridal dress with sleeves or a bridal dress with a train, your options will be more specific as to what you want to view. Also, if in your magazine search you find a designer who reflects a style that appeals to you, go directly to their website. Another suggestion is to look for bridal shows in your area that showcase wedding gowns. Make it a fun event to share with your mother, your girlfriends, or anyone you would enjoy getting involved in your wedding.

There are no limits to the number of different styles available to select from. Vintage, classic, contemporary, elegant, simple, sexy, glamorous, bows, ruffles, layers or any combination may be the perfect style for you. As you are a later in life bride, the dress can be any length. It can have long sleeves, short sleeves, capped sleeves or no sleeves at all. If sleeves are required by your religion or location, consider a dress that has sleeves which can be removed.

If you decide you want the glamour of a strapless gown or sexier bodice but are concerned this style isn't appropriate for the actual ceremony, there are solutions! Adding removable sleeves, a lace bodice, a bolero jacket or a shawl collar can make a dress still look fantastic but more demure. Some designers specifically create dresses for brides who want one look for the wedding and another for the reception. They construct their dresses to "convert" from a formal wedding dress to a party gown which is also a much easier and less costly solution than having two dresses.

Color can be your starting point. Do you want to wear a traditional white gown or are you interested in finding a pastel color? If you are a mature bride, you will probably find a softer version of white will complement your skin tones and be more flattering for your age. Tradition also dictates that ivory is more appropriate than white for a second wedding.

As a modern mature bride, you can bend the rules as long as you don't offend anyone. Even though the white dress has always been associated with a first marriage, we don't think anyone would consider it improper if you did not want to support this tradition. Wearing a white dress may be important to you, especially if you are a first time bride or feel that this marriage is your first formal ceremony because your last marriage was a simple courthouse affair.

The cost of your wedding dress will be a major budget item but you can find fabulous dresses in every style, from the simplest to the most elegant, in a wide range of prices. We suggest you do not try on dresses you can't afford because it will make it harder to get excited about a dress within your price range. If your sales associate does not ask you what your budget is, provide her (him) with this information so she doesn't waste both your time and energy. If at this point she still brings you gowns beyond your price range, you will know this bridal salon is not one you want to patronize. You don't necessarily need an expensive designer dress, however you do need a fabulous dress that makes you feel special. Remember, style is not determined by cost; it is determined by what looks best on you and what you feel comfortable wearing.

If you have budgetary restraints or not enough time to order a dress from a bridal salon or designer, think about looking for a wedding dress that is already made and you can purchase off-the-rack. Bridal stores also have floor samples or dresses that for some reason have been returned. However, under these circumstances it is more difficult to find a dress that is in good condition, in your size and color. Some brides wear borrowed dresses, have them made or make their own. You can also rent a wedding dress or look for a used one on the Internet. Any dress can be a wedding dress depending on your venue and the look you want to create. Just remember, you have to love your choice because it will always be a part of your wedding memories.

There are other factors to consider that may also influence the style of dress you select such as the geographic location of the wedding, the time of year, the time of day, whether indoors or outdoors, in a church, a private home or on the beach. When evaluating your dress options, it is important to consider what would be appropriate yet comfortable for your date and location. Some of your concerns might be your ability to easily move around in the dress, how heavy it is to wear or how difficult it would be to transport to your wedding venue.

A formal or traditional wedding may not be the style you and your fiancé have chosen to celebrate your marriage. Therefore the location of your wedding would have more influence on what you and Mr. Wonderful choose to wear. You may prefer to have a theme wedding such as cowboy western or a casual island affair. Therefore, you would want your dress to match that style. Or, you may want a wedding that reflects your family heritage or ethnic background. Some couples want to exchange their vows in a unique geographical location that has special memories for them. Some people have even gotten married under water!

Be cautious about surprising your groom on your wedding day by appearing in some unique style or costume. The image of how you look walking toward him down the aisle will be imprinted in his memory for the rest of his life. He will want to be proud of the choice he made in asking you to marry him and the first time he sees you as his bride is a very defining moment!

You don't need to have a wedding gown or a special dress if it isn't important to you or that isn't your style. Often a dressy pantsuit is more flattering on certain figures and can also be designed to look like a long dress by the way the pants flow as you walk. If you are considering a non-traditional wedding outfit, make certain it is a mutual decision that Mr. Wonderful enthusiastically supports. Don't assume your groom doesn't care. Remember, this is also a significant event in his life and he may have his own opinions and vision of his perfect wedding.

Before looking for your dress, answer these questions:

- What color do you want your dress to be?
- Do you want your dress to have sleeves?
- What neckline is most flattering on you?
- What fabrics do you like?
- Are there certain fabrics that are better for your location and season?
- Do you want your dress to be short, tea length or long?
- Do you prefer an A-line silhouette, an empire sheath, a slip dress or long, full, ball gown?
- Do you want a train, and if so, how long?
- Would you feel more comfortable in nice suit or pants outfit?

After you have narrowed down the style you think you want, write down all your thoughts, wishes and any options you may have found interesting. This will save you time and money in the long run. It is important to do your magazine and Internet research because you will be overwhelmed with the selections and styles available in the stores. Don't let the process of shopping for your gown overwhelm or intimidate you. You might be unprepared for the number of choices and become confused if you don't know what you are looking for.

No matter how busy or anxious you are, you must start looking for your dress within the limits of the timeline you have prepared. When you go into a store, immediately identify yourself as the bride. Communicate clearly with the sales staff what you are looking for and don't let anyone convince you to wear something designed for the mother-of-the-bride! If you have collected any pictures, show them to the sales associate and be as descriptive with the details as you can. With a dress concept in mind, it will be easy for you to eliminate a multitude of choices. The salesperson will be more attentive if you already know what styles you like and it will make the process of looking for your dress more enjoyable. Request a sales associate that is close to your age and has experience working with mature brides. She will be more apt to pay attention to your needs and make recommendations on what choices will be the most flattering for your figure. We don't want to discourage you from working with a younger salesperson. However, they may waste your time by offering selections that are trendy or more appealing to them rather than what is appropriate and flattering for your figure. No matter the age of your sales associate, keep an open mind to their suggestions. They have worked with a lot of brides, and after working with you and seeing the styles of dresses you are attracted to, you may be pleasantly surprised if she brings you a dress you never even considered a possibility!

If you know the exact style you are looking for, it is easy to glance through the gowns rather quickly but don't assume the selection of dresses you see on display represents the store's entire stock. You might consider taking a quick tour of the bridal salons in your area and then later making appointments at the stores which seem the most interesting. If you have an appointment, you have a better chance of getting personal attention and a salesperson to show you what is available in your style and price range. This is a unique shopping experience and you may feel slightly vulnerable or insecure but don't be shy when selecting and trying on dresses.

You intuitively know what looks best on you. But if you are not a shopper, and the thought of visiting several bridal stores or designer showrooms seems too stressful, ask a family member, friends or a personal shopper for their help. Make appointments at a few of the larger bridal salons so you can try on a variety of different styles to confirm the style you think you want is really the one that looks best on you. Don't forget to take a camera so you can review the dresses when you are done shopping. Don't be hasty. Prepare for this shopping experience to take a few days. You might also consider initially shopping alone before including other people who have their own ideas and opinions. You want to enjoy the process of deciding on your personal style and what looks great on you. So be thoughtful about who you want to invite to accompany you.

Everyone will want to be included in shopping for the dress and it is a great "girls' day." However, get organized and narrow down your choices before you invite your entire family and friends to participate in this shopping experience. Everyone loves to shop for wedding dresses and their choices may reflect what they like and not necessarily what looks best on you. So when you venture out to your selected bridal shops, be careful your friends are all people whose opinion you value. Don't make it an exhausting, negative experience by bringing in other "caring and interested" friends too early in the process.

Your body type, height and posture will strongly influence the style of dress that looks the most attractive on you. A beautiful dress you see in a magazine, or on the hanger in the store, may not be the most flattering style for your figure. Also, keep in mind the design of the dress because you want it to be a style that can be comfortably worn for many hours. Consider the weight of the fabric, its ability to move with you, and how it will flow as you walk down the aisle. Also pay special attention to the detail on the back of the dress because it is the view of your gown everyone will have during the ceremony. It will also be the view that will be captured in a lot of your wedding pictures and the vision most people will remember of the ceremony.

When finalizing the decision on your wedding gown, be conscious of how it fits. You know what looks best on your figure. Be honest with yourself. You can't change those hips or your body type. Respect and celebrate your age! The most important thing to remember and accept is the reality that your body may not be perfect and you are not a model presenting a designer collection. You know your body and what features you want to emphasize. Look for a dress that complements your figure while tastefully hiding some of your less attractive attributes - and don't worry - we all have them. Celebrate and be happy with your look! You might be able to lose a few pounds before the wedding, but don't count on it. Remember, you will have wonderful showers and celebrations leading up to your wedding.

Thank heavens for the new inventions the lingerie market has developed to accommodate our under garment challenges. Finding the correct bra, panties and slip are critical to your comfort and the complete look of the dress, especially from behind. Some dress styles lend themselves to having support built into the foundation of the dress to eliminate the need for traditional lingerie. Ask the designer or seamstress to work with you. Remember, no one will know what you don't have on. Be conscious of bulges or panty lines and don't hesitate to ask for help in resolving these problem areas.

The larger department stores have very knowledgeable sales associates. So, don't be shy! Tackle the problem head on. Only a very few women have a model's perfect body. The rest of us just need a little help. There are many options available and the Internet is a very personal and quick resource to help you find unusual lingerie in your size and to fit the design of your dress. Your goal is to make certain that your dress fits perfectly, flows smoothly over your body as you walk and most of all that you are comfortable and confident wearing it.

Do not hesitate to make appointments at designer showrooms. Purchasing a dress from an independent designer may not be any more expensive than buying a dress at a bridal store. Plus, they can be flexible with their designs to create a wedding dress that will be perfect for you. Seriously consider interviewing a designer if you want a dress that does not look like a traditional wedding gown or if you are looking for a dress that can be converted into another style for your reception. Other details to convey to your designer would be if you want a dress that can be modified after the wedding so you can wear it to other functions, or if you want a dress that no one will find in a bridal magazine and is uniquely your dress.

If you find a specific designer whose style appeals to you, ask for an appointment when the designer will be in the showroom. Use this opportunity to get to know the designer and develop a personal relationship with them so they can understand and create the look you want to achieve. A designer will intuitively know which styles and fabrics will be the most flattering on you and will make practical suggestions that you may never have considered. Designers can also compete with the price of a dress purchased at a bridal salon because they can adjust the cost by using different fabrics. They can also build into the dress the specific support features you need so you won't have to pay for additional alterations because the dress will be made for you. A designer's goal is to enhance a woman's own beauty. They are freer to adapt, adjust and do whatever it takes to make what you've created together into a fabulous dress designed just for your wedding.

Things to Consider When Trying on Your Dress

- How does it fit?
- Does the dress require special undergarments?
- Will it need alterations?
- How much will the alterations cost?
- Is the dress comfortable?
- Can you dance gracefully in the dress?
- Is the dress heavy?
- Will the dress be too hot to wear for a long time?
- If the dress is beaded, can you sit down comfortably without damaging the beading detail?
- If the dress is strapless, can you support it without constantly making adjustments?
- If the dress has straps, can you tape them in place?
- Are you looking for a dress that will accommodate a specific piece of jewelry you want to wear?

It is important that you stay in charge of the decision and purchase. As unusual as it may seem, you must also be prepared to negotiate the terms of the purchase of your dress. By politely defining and agreeing to the purchase details when ordering the dress, you will minimize confrontations and expenses you were not prepared to pay for down the road. Especially at a time when other decisions need to be made and you have already exceeded your budget. If your dress requires alterations, do not neglect to ask what these charges will be up front. Also, be aware there may be add-on charges for ironing the dress or if you request an early delivery date. You don't want to jeopardize the joy of finding the ideal dress by neglecting the details involved in the purchase price.

Once you find the perfect dress, decide if you want to keep it a secret or if you would like the opinion of a close friend or relative. It can be a special decision shared by a mother and daughter, father, favorite uncle, or close friend. However, you may want to wait for everyone to see you in your dress for the first time when you walk down the aisle as a bride. The choice is yours. Either way, the first time a loved one sees you in your wedding dress is quite an emotional moment because of how beautiful you look and what that moment symbolizes to them.

Choosing your dress is a major element in defining your style. However, there are still many more decisions that you have to make associated with your dress to complete the look you want to accomplish. We will have a discussion about accessories in a later chapter, but when deciding on your wedding gown or outfit, you should keep the following accessories in mind:

- What kind of shoes do you want to wear?
- What hairstyle would look best?
- Do you want to wear hair ornaments?
- Do you want to wear a tiara?
- Do you want to wear a veil?
- Did the designer of your gown also design a specific veil to go with it?

- Do you want a dress with a train?
- Do you want to wear gloves?
- What kind of jewelry would go well with the gown or outfit you have chosen to wear?
- Do you need a wrap or shawl?

Another thing to decide is how you are going to transport the dress. This is an important detail to consider no matter if your wedding is local or if you are planning a destination wedding. Have a conversation with your wedding coordinator, or the sales associate at the store where you purchased the gown, for the best and safest way to get the dress to your wedding venue. One option is for the store to ship the dress to a specific location (hotel, friend, etc.) ahead of time and select an individual who will assume the responsibility of keeping the dress until you arrive. If you are traveling on an airplane, consult your specific carrier about their guidelines. We do not recommend you pack your wedding dress in your checked luggage and assume it will arrive with you. It is better to hand carry it on to the plane and hang it somewhere safe where you can keep an eye on it. Whatever the circumstances of your wedding location, you should be in charge of your dress while traveling or arrange to have it sent to the location before you arrive. You don't want to add more stress to your wedding by worrying about where your dress is. The comfort and security of having your dress with you, pressed and ready to wear on the morning of your wedding, will relieve any additional anxiety.

Planning a wedding can be a very tense, nervous and exciting time and you may be amazed how much attention is put on the bridal gown. However, once you start trying on dresses you will understand. Ultimately, you will find the final decision very simple because when you find the right dress you will know it. You will feel confident and wonderful about how you look and all the rest of the accessories and details associated with your style will fall into place. Your goal is to have fun making all the decisions and to feel fabulous and comfortable with your choices.

ACCESSORIZING YOUR STYLE

Accessorizing your dress can sometimes be more difficult than finding your dress! Do you want to wear gloves, jewelry, a hair ornament or tiara? There are abundant opportunities to add accessories to make your style more interesting and complete.

Shoes

It is critically important to find comfortable shoes! There is nothing more crucial than having happy feet the day of your wedding. Although stilettos are fun to wear, it is far better to find a beautiful, practical alternative. In our youth we would put up with just about any pain in order to wear the most gorgeous, stylish shoes we could find. The pain was worth the fabulous look. However, with maturity we understand that comfort is more important than style. You don't want to grimace throughout your wedding just hoping to have the ceremony end so you can take off your shoes. Be conscious of finding the perfect pair of shoes that will be comfortable for your entire wedding celebration.

If you do happen to fall completely head over heels for a pair of shoes that you know will turn on you before your wedding celebration is over, we do have a solution. Buy another pair of shoes to change into when you need a break from the perfect but painful shoes you couldn't resist. And remember to have someone place them under the table for you so they are easily accessible when you need them.

We also think you should consider specialized shoes made for ballroom dancing. They are the perfect solution for beautiful shoes you can wear into the night and even through the last dance. With the popularity of "Dancing with the Stars" and other dance competition events on television, different styles of beautiful dancing shoes are becoming more available.

Matching your shoes to your dress and the location of your ceremony often has its challenges. You won't be looking for the same style of shoe for a church wedding as you would for a wedding on the beach or on a grassy hillside. For instance, marrying on the sand, a grass walkway, or in someone's home requires shoes that allow you to gracefully walk up and down stairs, move securely on uneven surfaces, and will stay on your feet even if they get caught on your hem or your heel gets stuck in the grass. You don't want to trip, lose your balance or even lose a shoe. That might be entertainment for your guests, but not a good memory for either you or Mr. Wonderful. So our advice is to focus on buying attractive, comfortable, practical shoes so you won't have to worry about someone catching you in a photo wincing because your feet hurt.

Break in your shoes well in advance of your wedding. The best time is at the end of one of your busy days when your feet are already tired and swollen. If your shoes feel too tight, go to your favorite shoe repair store and have them stretched overnight. Then revisit your plan of trying them on after a busy day. As we have suggested, it is advisable to plan on two pairs of shoes for your wedding event just in case one pair becomes unbearably uncomfortable.

Also prepare for foot emergencies and include bandages, creams and soothing foot balm in your "Bridal Rescue Kit". Another important detail to remember is that you may be too excited to realize how painful your feet are becoming as your wedding progresses. So a word to the wise, don't take your shoes off when you finally get to sit down unless you have planned to have a second pair. Chances are you won't be sitting long before someone comes to your table to give you their congratulations. At that point, you might not be able to put your shoes back on! Remember, if your feet are uncomfortable they will distract you from fully enjoying your special day.

The length of your dress and height of the groom are also important considerations when choosing your shoes. When your dress is long, don't dismiss the idea of glamorized tennis shoes, flip-flops or colorful rhinestone sandals. Especially if the terrain at the ceremony is challenging or you are taller than Mr. Wonderful. If your dress is short, you may think about customized dance shoes or a high, strappy sandal that will make you look taller and your legs longer. When your groom is tall, platform shoes might be a beautiful and fashionable alternative. If he is close to your stature, be sensitive to his feelings about your comparative heights. Sometimes this is more of an issue for him at the altar. You can always change to higher heels later during the reception.

All of your choices are appropriate in creating your own personal style, but remember comfort is the key component and no one will be looking at your feet! They are focusing on you and the happiness you radiant through-out your wedding celebration.

After choosing the location of your event, evaluate the surface where you will be walking down the aisle. Extremely high heels will penetrate most grassy areas, even if you have a protective, decorative runner. An uneven surface will slow the procession to a halt, especially if you get stuck! This also applies to your attendants' shoes. Most facilities that specialize in weddings have anticipated this problem, and will provide a special, harder surface that can be covered with a decorative runner. As you can imagine, tripping as you go down the aisle may be distracting and challenging for both you and your attendants. It can also be an embarrassing and an unnecessary distraction during the ceremony. As the bride, you want to glide down the aisle with grace and style without worrying about your next step.

Make-Up
The key to completing your wedding look is to accentuate your best features and you achieve this with the proper use and amount of makeup.

You may not be comfortable having someone else do your make-up because the look they achieve is usually more dramatic than you are comfortable with on a daily basis. Your wedding day is different. Your make-up has to last for hours and you will be having hundreds of pictures taken which requires a more defined, elegant or dramatic look. Extend your comfort level and schedule a professional makeup consultation to help you evaluate and update your appearance.

Look for a make-up consultant not just a make-up artist. All too often, cosmeticians create a dramatic look which may make you feel too "made-up". A good makeup consultant will give you a fresh, radiant look that you will feel comfortable wearing all year round. Not just on your wedding day. They will also guide and encourage you to experiment with different ideas so you will know how to make your appearance more dramatic for special occasions. The proper use of make-up can make you look stunning and dramatic as well as natural and relaxed.

You will also want to create a look that will last for hours without getting shiny from nerves or heat. It will be a long day even if you have an evening wedding. The color palette and type of makeup you choose will depend on the location of your ceremony, the time of year, the time of day, and the color of your dress. Learning about make-up, and your "look", takes time so don't delay this part – it is a fun experience and your girlfriends will enjoy doing this with you!

Before you start experimenting with make-up, evaluate the condition and shape of your eyebrows. Eyebrows define your face, emphasize your eyes and have a huge impact on your look. If you have sparse eyebrows, you can learn how to fill them in with an eyebrow pencil. Waxing your eyebrows will give them additional color and definition.

The first cosmetic product you need to identify is the primer which creates a base for your foundation and will help your makeup stay fresh longer. It also plumps up your skin to give it a smoother texture, minimizes your pores, and makes your fine lines look less obvious. After the primer, you need to find a lightweight, liquid mineral or cream foundation that has light-reflecting properties. This product will also smooth the appearance of fine lines, cover irregular pigmentation and give your complexion an even appearance. However, be careful not to overdue your foundation as it might become "masklike" and be sure to blend it in thoroughly. Complete the foundation with a light powder and a blush. Depending on your skin tone, a light pink blush is often the best choice as it will appear more radiant and glowing on your skin. Now you are ready for the fun part – your eye make-up!

If your idea of glamour is smoky eyes, then try them out! However, don't be too trendy. To give depth to your eyes and make them stand out, use an eyeliner. This will also make your lashes look fuller and your eyes brighter. Often a dark blue or purple liner is complimentary for any color of eyes. Eye shadows are also a fun way to play with color around your eyes but be careful using overly frosted tints because they tend to overstate their presence. You will look your most alluring with understated eye shadows that won't overpower your features. We recommend lightly shimmery hues of copper and gold that will make your eyes sparkle without seeming to be overly made up. A soft white shade under your brow bone will also make your eyes appear fresh, open and uplifted. To play up your glamorous eyes, you will want to balance the rest of your make-up with neutral colors and a hint of pink of course!

Your wedding is a very emotional time and there may be tears so plan ahead and purchase waterproof mascara. A light black, brown-black or blue mascara as well as adding false eyelashes will give your lashes a rich appearance. The whites of your eyes will also appear more pronounced. Also, don't forget to use an eyelash conditioner under your mascara especially if you use an eyelash curler.

Your lips are one of your most prominent features, so it is important that you pay attention to your lipstick during the entire wedding event. Your face make-up will stay set and can be touched up quickly with a soft brushing of powder, but lipsticks fade so be prepared to refresh them often. A rose-colored creamy lipstick topped with a hint of gloss will brighten your lips better than a matte color. If you use a lip-gloss, make sure it is not sticky and wears well. An underlying application of lip stain will also help retain your lip color.

Assign one of your attendants to carry a little purse with your lipstick, lip-gloss, lip liner and lip conditioner, and make it her responsibility to alert you when your lip color needs attention. If you want fuller lips, there are lip plumpers on the market; you can also apply concealers and conditioners around your mouth to soften small lines. For photos, choose a vibrant shade of lipstick, again in a rose tone instead of taupe; avoid beige or pale colors as they have a tendency to make you look tired. For your teeth to look their brightest, plan ahead and have them professionally whitened or use a whitening tooth product for several weeks prior to the wedding.

If you are going to have your make-up done by a consultant on the day of your wedding, it is ideal to have a trial make-up session on the same day as you have your pre-wedding hair appointment. This way you can see the complete look and make any adjustments if necessary. Try to plan this at least two to three weeks before your wedding.

If the makeup consultant is not going to be on site at your wedding, make sure you have a duplicate set of the cosmetics she used to achieve your look so you can touch up your make-up if necessary. If you decide to do your own make-up, you should practice applying your cosmetics several times in lighting similar to what you will experience the day of your event. When you are confident you can achieve the look you want by applying your own make-up, wear it for several hours and have someone take your picture. This test will confirm whether or not you understand what is involved in applying your own make-up the day of your wedding – and don't forget to put "back up" Cosmetics in your "Bridal Rescue Kit".

Mr. Wonderful may seem perfectly happy with the way you are now, but with a little careful preparation and the right make-up techniques, you can subtly enhance your features. Your groom may think you look a little different but not know exactly why; what is important is that you look incredibly fantastic, happy and relaxed.

Hair
Make a hair plan! Your hairstyle and hair accessories must complete the look of your dress and not compete with it.

Planning ahead for how you want to wear your hair will give you time to experiment with new styles and looks. Hair stylists can do amazing things when you feel comfortable enough to get out of your box and try something new. However, you may have become accustomed to a hairstyle you have comfortably worn for a long time and Mr. Wonderful likes it. And at this time, you don't want to change this look because you think it will be easier for you to manage and you have already made your veil and/or hair ornament decisions around this style. But then again, this may be the perfect time for you to try a totally new look for which you must plan ahead.

You may want to grow your hair longer or experiment with several different styles. If you have always wanted to have long hair piled on top of your head with flowers, a veil, sparkling jewels or a headpiece, make sure this is the look you convey to your hairdresser. However, understand that many traditional up-do's can be more aging and severe if not done properly.

Not all hairdressers are professionally prepared to create a hairstyle for a wedding. Your hairstyle has to last for hours so you will need to find a stylist that is versatile and has experience producing styles that can support hair ornaments, flowers, a veil or a tiara. Take the time to interview them to make sure they understand the "look" you are trying to achieve. Also be clear about the time commitment you expect from them. You may want them to provide a pre-wedding appointment and also be with you the day of the wedding. Some brides are comfortable having their hair done at the salon before the wedding while other brides want their stylist with them during their entire wedding event.

If yours is a destination wedding, get several recommendations for hair stylists from your wedding coordinator, the hotel or the Internet. Contact them ahead of time and conduct a phone interview. Ask if they have a website which previews some of the wedding hairstyles they have created for other brides. Once you have identified some hairstyles you like, take advantage of your local stylist to practice creating the hairstyles that appeal to you. When you and your local stylist achieve the look you have been hoping for, take digital pictures and email them to your destination stylist. Follow up with a phone call to discuss your plan together and if they have any suggestions or think there are some adjustments that have to be made due to the climate, the style of your dress or the location of the wedding. It is critical to have your hair done at least 3 weeks to a month prior to the wedding to be certain you love the style and it is not just a creative whim of you or the hairdresser. Also, if you decide to have your hair cut, and it is cut a little too short, having your hair styled a few weeks before the wedding will give you time to let it grow out. This period of time will also allow your cut to relax and soften a bit. A great cut is one that lets your hair move but has memory and plays up your best features. If you are having your hair colored, allow about a week for the color to blend in and calm down so it will look more naturally attractive.

If the style you want requires hair extensions, ask the stylist which method they use to attach the hairpieces and if they can purchase the extensions for you. It is also advisable to experiment wearing extensions several months in advance of your wedding to make sure you like the "look" and you can wear them comfortably.

Bring your veil, hair ornaments, pictures of your dress and pictures of the hairstyles you like to your appointment so the stylist knows the look you want to achieve. If you don't feel confident about this person or they can't interpret your style the way you want it to be, you must try another stylist. This will take time and energy on your part. However, it is worth paying attention to this detail in order be certain you can bring together all the hair style elements you have envisioned. This is the only way you will be sure to achieve the wedding look you have always dreamed of.

If you already have your dress and it is easily transported, take it with you to your hair appointment so you can hold it up or carefully slip it on. This will allow you to see the complete look you have created with your dress, jewelry, hair and make-up. It will also allow you the opportunity to make any last minute adjustments. If your normal stylist is not available the day of the wedding, have them take pictures and make notes of the steps involved when creating your hairstyle.

Take time to walk around and wear your new hairstyle for several hours after your appointment to see how it holds up to time and temperature, especially if it is an up do. This is important because this is when you will need to address any issues that are not consistent with the look you want to achieve. Be prepared to make any minor hair adjustments you did not anticipate because of the location, your dress, your accessories, and most of all, your comfort throughout the event. Keep in mind, if you are getting married in a steamy or humid environment, your head will get hot sooner and you will melt a bit faster. Address all of your hair concerns with your hair stylist ahead of time. Be absolutely certain you are completely thrilled and you look like the bride you have always envisioned yourself to be. Remember, this is the wedding of your dreams. If your hair isn't exactly the way you want it, you will be distracted throughout the entire event and unhappy when you see your wedding pictures later on! On your wedding day, you don't want to be in the position of redoing a hairstyle you don't like or has fallen out. If your hair isn't the way you want it, you'll continue to fuss with it, get annoyed and it will influence your self-confidence. It is critical that you love your hair because it frames your face and everyone will be looking at you! *Don't compromise!*

Always remember, there is nothing worse than having a bad hair day at your wedding!

The Veil

Does your fantasy bridal dress include a veil? That all depends on you!

Of course you can have a veil at any age and one of the authors did! Presenting yourself to your groom under a veil is steeped in tradition. The moment when the bride is presented and the veil is lifted is a memory shared by everyone, especially the bride and groom. Although not essential, it is very traditional and very romantic. If you are getting married later in life, you may not want to wear a veil because it is not appropriate for long standing rules of etiquette, the location, the theme of your wedding, or your own personal style. However, if you want to wear a veil, it should be considered at the time you are selecting your dress. When deciding on and selecting a veil, evaluate the type of fabric and design of your dress. The length of your hair will also be a factor because it must be styled in such a way to support the weight of the veil.

There are many ways to wear a veil, and if you decide you want to wear one, it doesn't have to go over your face. Your veil can be short, fingertip length or long so it flows gracefully down the back of your dress. After the ceremony you can continue to wear your veil, you can bustle it for convenience or you can take it off. However, if you decide you are going to take your veil off after the ceremony, you should work with your hairdresser in advance so you fully understand how you are going to manage your hair once the veil is removed. If your hairdresser is not on site after the ceremony, be sure that you, or one of your attendants, can style your hair quickly so you will be pleased with how you look in your pictures and for the rest of your wedding celebration. There is nothing more upsetting than the thought of "hat hair" on your wedding day!

Tiaras and Hair Ornaments
A tiara looks good on any woman at any age and you can combine one with a veil!

Tiaras and hair ornaments are accessories that can be a unique and creative way to make a style statement but choose something elegant yet tasteful that does not distract from your overall appearance. You can spend a little or a lot of money on hair accessories by either purchasing them or creating your own. If you decide to make your own, there are bead and fabric stores everywhere and the staff is always available to help you find what you need. It is easier to communicate what you are looking for if you have pictures or drawings, so don't forget to take them with you. If you want a tiara or hair ornament but don't have the budget to purchase one or the time and interest to make your own, don't forget to look for what you want at an inexpensive costume jewelry store in the mall. Also, research the Internet or see if you can find someone who will make the hair accessory for you.

If you want something else to add to your hairstyle that isn't as traditional and formal as a veil, or as fancy and sparkling as a tiara, you might consider flowers. A simple flower accent may be a stunning choice. Artificial flowers may be a smart alternative to fresh flowers due to the location of the wedding and length of your celebration. The natural heat of your head may cause real flowers to wilt which would be embarrassing. If you want to embellish your look with a veil, a tiara, hair ornaments or a headpiece with flowers, go for it!

Gloves

Gloves are a personal decision, which may be quite stylish and complete your look.

The style of your dress, the location of your wedding, and the time of year will help you make the decision of whether or not to wear gloves. If you want to wear gloves, anticipate the process of removing the glove from your left hand for the ring ceremony. Then decide if you are going to put the glove back on, and if so, how you are going to do it gracefully? Practice taking them off and on until it looks effortless, casual and glamorous. Remember to take them to your wedding rehearsal so both you and Mr. Wonderful are prepared for what the gloves involve when you exchange rings. You can also buy gloves specially designed for the ring ceremony which have a section on the left hand ring finger that is detachable. This is an alteration that can also be done by your local seamstress.

Jewelry

Jewelry can be a very confusing style element to try and work with or around.

You may want to wear a special family heirloom for sentimental reasons or your dress may dictate the need for the drama of jewelry by its design. Be careful. Too much jewelry, or the wrong style of jewelry, can detract from your dress and the total look you are trying to achieve. Rhinestone necklaces and tiaras are currently very popular but they may not work with the style of your dress, especially if it is already heavily decorated.

If you are purchasing jewelry, be sure to only buy pieces that can be returned. Understand the stores return policy since you may have to try several different pieces of jewelry with the dress before you can make a decision. Also, have the jewelry with you on the day of your pre-wedding hair and make-up appointment. The look of your earrings, necklace and veil, as well as the neckline of your dress, are important for the hairdresser to see before you both make a decision on how you want your hair styled for your wedding. After this appointment, you will definitely know if the jewelry complements you and the style of your dress. You are the bride and you will be glowing with happiness and love. Be careful not to detract from that image.

Wrap or Shawl

Don't forget to include a cover-up or shawl on your shopping list.

No matter what the location and time of year, the weather cools down throughout the day. You may also get tired which can make you more sensitive to the cooler temperature and air conditioning will also be a factor. Finding the perfect cover-up for your dress may be more difficult than you think. Start looking once you have decided on what you are going to wear to your wedding. A simple Pashmina shawl or wrap similar to your train is an easy solution. If your dress is white, you may even want to jazz it up with a colored or embroidered alternative.

Just remember, it is not about the accessory but the style you are trying to create.

Style Notes:

CHAPTER FOUR

THE FIFTEEN MOST SIGNIFICANT

Details

AND QUIZZES

Details

This wedding is your dream come true so evaluate your resources and make choices that fulfill your fantasy or vision for that day.

We have listed the fifteen most significant wedding categories you need to focus on when planning your wedding. This list does not indicate where you should spend the most money but instead will help you determine where you should focus your time and resources in creating your own personal style. Of the fifteen most significant wedding categories, we feel location, date and dress are the most important. However, deciding whether or not to hire a wedding consultant is also an important early decision you should consider.

WHERE TO START

The best way to start planning your wedding is to make a list of all the fundamental decisions that have to be made and list them in the order of what is most important to each of you. Consider the expense of each item as secondary at this point. We have found the first decision most couples make is where they would like to get married. Once the location has been determined, the date can be set. When these critical decisions have been made, it gets easier. The fun begins and you get to look for your dress!

The most wonderful thing about getting married at this time of your life is you can create the wedding of your dreams without feeling obligated to follow the traditions found in wedding manuals that tell you what to do and when. However, with the opportunity to design a wedding that fits your style, always be sensitive to your guests and their religious and social expectations so as not to offend anyone with your choices. You, Mr. Wonderful, your budget and the people with whom you want to share this very intimate, special day are the only limitations to your wedding dreams.

In our opinion, as well as those of other modern mature brides whom we have interviewed, your location and dress are the most important elements to showing off your style. We also think stationery is equally important. Your style will be obvious throughout all of the elements of your wedding event. Through networking with friends and family, and the unlimited number of resources available on the Internet, you can reasonably turn your creative ideas into reality. Now you need to establish a budget. Money is always a sensitive subject and you need to thoughtfully prepare a budget in order to start planning your wedding. You need to discuss who is going to pay for what part of the wedding and how much they willing to contribute. We know it is a difficult subject to broach, especially as a woman getting married later in life. However, completely paying for your wedding may be something you can't finance on your own. Discuss it with Mr. Wonderful and your family so you can evaluate all your resources. You can't start making wedding plans until you decide on a budget and allocate how much you are going to spend in each area. Once your budget is established, you can start comfortably planning and making decisions.

Identifying the Fifteen Most Significant Wedding Details

1. Location
2. Date
3. Bridal Party
4. The Dress
5. The Guest List
6. Wedding Coordinator
7. Stationery
8. Website
9. Ceremony
10. Officiate
11. Reception

12. Photographer and/or Videographer

13. Flowers and Décor

14. Rehearsal or Pre-wedding Reception

15. Honeymoon

LOCATION
is the Most Important Detail

Deciding on the location of your wedding will impact many other decisions such as the style of your dress, your shoes, the flowers, the number of people you can invite, and so many other unforeseen details. This is when hiring a local wedding coordinator is a good investment because she will make you aware of all your options and help you recognize all the details involved in the location you eventually choose.

Location may not necessarily be determined by convenience. One important consideration when making this decision is to decide if you want a destination wedding or one close to home. One problem associated with a modern, mature bride is that you may have been raised, gone to school or had a career in several different places all of which you have identified as home at one time or another. So, you will have to decide what will be the perfect location for your wedding. Is it the home where you were raised, where you live now, where most of your family and friends live or where your fiancé has roots?

The time of year, as well as the day of the week and time of day will also impact your decision about the wedding location. If finances are a consideration, planning your wedding on a Friday or Sunday will dramatically reduce the cost. Also, getting married in the mid-morning or early afternoon is usually less expensive than an evening wedding. Once you both decide on the geographical location of your ceremony, you can focus on the specific issues such as whether your wedding will be in a church, hotel, restaurant or historic site and whether it will be indoors or outdoors. When making these choices consider the time of year, time of day, number of anticipated guests and accessibility for caterers and other vendors. However, the most important consideration for determining the where and when of your wedding event is how much you have allocated to spend.

Destination Weddings

Sometimes all of your choices make a destination wedding an easy compromise. With a destination wedding, you can choose a location that is convenient to most of the people you want to attend your wedding ceremony. It could be a fabulous, far away location or a place close to home that will provide memories of a lifetime for everyone involved. When we were younger, where our friends and family lived usually determined where the ceremony was performed. Today, most of us have family and friends spread throughout the world and they now have access and the ability to travel almost anywhere. However, we will caution you on one point. If you plan a destination wedding thinking a lot of people won't come, remember friends and family love an excuse to travel and many of them will decide to make your wedding a family vacation! So this is the time to limit your guest list and other major wedding decisions to what you can really afford.

The location of your wedding may also be dictated by the time of year you want to get married. You may want to get married in the summer on the beach with your feet in the water but other commitments indicate a winter wedding makes more sense. Therefore, to make your dream come true you need to find a beach location that is warm during the winter months of the year such as California, Arizona, Hawaii, Costa Rica, Florida or the Caribbean to name a few.

There are other options to consider if you want to make the dream of your destination wedding come true. You can plan a smaller wedding and keep the guest list to family and close friends. Or, choose a destination that is closer and an easy distance to drive to. Try not to plan your wedding during a busy holiday, which will increase travel expenses for everyone and will probably add to the cost of the venue. Research if your destination offers wedding packages, or consider a more economical "hometown' wedding and go to a warm beach location for your honeymoon!

Indoor versus Outdoor Weddings

Indoor weddings are easier to plan because the environment is more predictable. But, depending on the room, indoor weddings may either require more expense or imagination to make the venue unique to your style.

Outdoor weddings usually require more attention to detail but allow more flexibility with cost. The vendors can be arranged for separately which will eliminate a separate facility charge. If your outdoor wedding is at a commercial venue, which provides most of the standard furniture and fixtures, there may be hidden costs (or "plus-pluses" as they are called) added to the food and beverages beyond the standard facility charge.

Compile a detailed list of the cost for each vendor before you decide on a complete facility package or an independent venue where you contract with private vendors. If you have an outdoor, creative wedding, it is helpful to use a caterer or rental company who will provide all the necessities like tables, chairs, linens, etc. In the final analysis, you may save a considerable amount of time, money and worry if you use a commercial facility.

If you are not having a church wedding, be certain the information you provide for your guests is clear regarding the physical location of each event on your wedding day so they are prepared for the possibility of sand, sun, wind, steps, etc. Be ready for complicating weather factors by providing umbrellas, a tent, or an awning for shade or rain. Have chairs available for elderly people or children who tire of standing quickly. It is very important and considerate to provide bathroom facilities if your wedding is on the beach or at an outdoor venue far away from an established building or structure.

When planning an outdoor wedding, consider an indoor alternative, or a tent, so your wedding won't be ruined if the weather becomes inclement. Also, provide some type of refreshment while your guests are waiting for everyone to arrive and the ceremony to begin. Depending on the time of your wedding, you may not want to serve alcohol too early in the festivities because the effect of being in the sun and drinking may catch some of your guests off guard. We have heard some brides mention they don't want any alcohol before the wedding because they want to keep everyone "in the moment" for the ceremony, and let the party start at the reception. Therefore, water or light fruit punches are good choices.

It may seem glamorous or romantic to get married at a unique location, and it often is, but think seriously about the complications you might encounter and prepare for them. This is another reason to hire a wedding coordinator and to select one who has previously done a wedding at the location you have chosen. As an example, if you choose a beach location you will need a microphone so your vows can be heard over the sound of the waves. If you have a sound system, it must be wireless or you will need some source of electricity for a standard system.

There are so many emotional things you have to deal with on your wedding day which makes it critical you manage, anticipate and delegate. Coordinate all the last minute details with your wedding consultant or someone you have designated to handle issues that might complicate your wedding day. Try to think of everything that can go wrong - and plan for it! Attention to detail in the initial stages of preparing for your wedding will eliminate a lot of anxiety on the day of your wedding.

Church Weddings

Having a church wedding is less complicated because the facility usually has a basic program they expect you to follow depending on the religious traditions or regulations of the denomination. They may also require the bride to use their in in-house wedding coordinator who is familiar with the church's wedding procedures and will make certain their guidelines are followed correctly. This person is someone who will instruct everyone before, during and after the ceremony; some of these details will include when to walk down the aisle, where to stand at the altar, and what each person's responsibilities are in the wedding program. The church coordinator will be there throughout the entire process and will help arrange the specifics of the ceremony. Since you did not get to interview or choose this individual who is going to manage one of the most important parts of your wedding, keep an open line of communication with them and work on arranging the specifics of the ceremony together. This person has seen a lot of weddings and experienced a lot of brides' personalities, some of whom may have been more demanding, impolite, unreliable, self-centered and demanding than others. The type of relationship you will have with this person is up to you. They will want you to have the wedding of your dreams and will work with you to fit in your personal preferences if they are within the guidelines of the church.

The church coordinator will be your advocate if you treat them with respect. You may wonder why we have been so direct regarding this issue. It is because we have many friends who represent their churches as wedding coordinators. Their experiences are usually wonderful. However, sometimes they can't wait to get the bride down the aisle and to her reception where someone else is in charge. Even though you did not choose the person the church has instructed you to work with, they are on your team. Respect the individual in charge and understand there are rules the church has given them to follow. As with all the people you work with, be courteous, on time with your appointments and cooperate with all people related to the church and involved in your service. They understand this is a very emotional and personal time and they will do all they can to make it a perfect wedding ceremony for you and your guests. If you have a problem accepting or understanding their rules, remember they have helped many, many brides walk up the aisle.

DATE
is the Second Most Important Detail

The date is important in establishing your timeline and the style of your wedding. The location and time of year will determine what kind of weather you will experience and must plan around. Choosing the height of the season in certain warm weather locations may also be more expensive than having the ceremony slightly off-season in the months when the weather might be less predictable. Deciding on your dress style and accessories will also revolve around the time of year. So don't fall in love with a dress before the date and location are firmly set!

BRIDAL PARTY
is the Third Most Important Detail

Choosing who you want to stand up for you at your wedding is a very important decision. The number of people you want in your wedding party may also be a factor in where you will have your wedding. And if you want a lot of attendants, does Mr. Wonderful have the same number of people to support him at the altar? It is an honor to be asked to stand up for someone at their marriage but with this honor comes a major expense and time commitment. If you want to include a lot of family or friends in your ceremony, first discuss it with Mr. Wonderful to get his input. If you have to eliminate some friends and family members who assumed they would be a part of your wedding party, be sensitive to their disappointment. Spend some time with them and explain why you were not able to include them.

Being a modern mature bride, you may not want to have an entourage of attendants. The matron or maid of honor is someone who is dear to your heart, will be your main confidant in planning your wedding and will be there for you before, during and after the ceremony. She is the one who will hold your bridal bouquet and groom's ring during the ceremony. She will attend to all your needs the day of your wedding and will help with other last minute details. She will arrange your dress and

---

Location Quiz for Couples

- Where do you want to be married?
- What time of year do you want to be married?
- What time of the day do you want to be married?
- Do you want a church wedding or a non-denominational location?
- What style ceremony do you want?
- How many people do you want to invite to your wedding?

---

accessories as well as your change of clothes and going away outfit. She will also stand in the receiving line and propose a toast to you and Mr. Wonderful. If you choose both a matron and maid of honor, the maid of honor will always take preference and will be the witness to your vows and signing of the marriage certificate.

Some men don't nurture a large circle of close friends as they get older and it may be awkward for your groom to identify and ask several men to stand up for him. If Mr. Wonderful has children, he may want them to be his attendants. The people you ask to be in your wedding party do not have to be limited by age, relationship or gender. Marsha had her sons as her attendants and Mike had his daughters. But keep in mind, it is an honor to be asked to be in someone's weddings and you should only give this honor to someone that is important to you and will appreciate and respect the privilege you have bestowed on them. When we were younger, and less thoughtful and mature, we chose our bridesmaids based on more social issues: who was our best friend, who had asked us to be in their wedding, who could afford to buy the dress and do the parties, and other criteria that was important at that time of our life. But now we have a different perspective of our wedding and what it means to be included in the wedding party. Think carefully about who and why you are asking someone to be your attendant because it should be someone who is important in your life now and you hope will always be a part of your married life with Mr. Wonderful.

Your Groom may ask his eldest brother, eldest son or best friend to stand up for him. The best man is responsible for helping the groom coordinate any rental clothing and takes care of returning the clothing after the wedding. He is responsible for holding the bride's wedding ring and delivers the fee to the Officiate. He will provide the first toast to you as a couple at the reception but he is not obligated to stand in your receiving line. He will also be responsible for arranging the transportation you will need to leave the reception. However, his primary duty is getting Mr. Wonderful ready for the wedding and making certain that he arrives at the ceremony on time!

The ushers' primary responsibilities are to seat all the guests and family members. If your wedding is large, it is wise to appoint a head usher who directs the other ushers as to where to seat the guests.

Attendants may include:
Maid &/or Matron of Honor
Bridesmaid(s)
Junior Bridesmaid(s)
Flower Girl(s)
Best Man
Groomsmen
Ushers
Ring Bearer

Having Your Children in Your Wedding

If you or Mr. Wonderful have children from previous marriages, include them as much as possible in your wedding plans. Depending on their age, they can be flower girls, ring bearers, bridesmaids, ushers, junior attendants, the best man, the maid of honor, or your escort down the aisle! Flower girls and ring bearers are usually between three and seven years old. The flower girls usually carry a basket or bouquet of flowers which can be scattered on the path for the bride. The ring bearer carries the ring or rings which are usually displayed on a white pillow. However, if they are very young, most couples choose to have their main attendants be responsible for their rings and have simulated wedding rings attached to the pillow for effect. Junior ushers and bridesmaids range in age between eight and fourteen because they are too old to be flower girls and ring bearers and yet too young to be bridesmaids and ushers. Their main responsibility is to walk in the procession behind the bridesmaids and ushers. The opportunity to have your children in your wedding can be adapted depending on the age of your children and how much you want them to be involved.

In addition, children can also perform special readings, sing a song, play an instrument or light a candle during the service. You can even include them when you are saying your wedding vows.

Having your children escort you down the aisle is a very special memory to share with each other. It use to be that only a Bride's Father or an older family relative or friend could escort a bride down the aisle. Today, it is perfectly acceptable to have one or two daughters or sons escort you down the aisle. It is also appropriate for you to walk alone if you want this moment to be exclusively yours.

Your wedding is all about you and the blending of your families. Remember, as a bride you are the focus of the day. At this time of your life you don't need to add friends to your ceremony just to make them feel included in your wedding or to repay them for asking you to be in their wedding. Everyone will be thrilled just to be invited and to witness your happiness.

DRESS & ACCESSORIES
are the Fourth Most Important Details

The dress as we mentioned is one of the most important decisions you will make in creating your own unique wedding style. The dress you select may be partially determined by its cost and the location you have chosen. You will find that some bridal stores categorize their gowns by either price or season. So be focused, be disciplined, and try to only look at the dresses you can realistically afford. Your accessories and any necessary alterations may increase the total cost, so keep this in mind when planning your budget.

If you find the perfect dress but it is beyond your budget, revisit your dress budget and see where you can cut your expenses. Some suggestions might be making your own hair ornaments, veil or headpiece or taking your dress to a regular seamstress for alternations rather than using the bridal store's tailor.

We all know how important the dress is so we have given "The Dress" special attention in another chapter!

GUEST LIST
is the Fifth Most Important Detail

One of the most challenging tasks for any couple is who to invite, especially when blending families. It is important to be sensitive to your respective children and former relatives. Many later-in-life weddings are small, private ceremonies which only include the family and close friends followed by a reception after the wedding or honeymoon.

When Elizabeth and her Mr. Wonderful chose to get married, they decided to marry on the East Coast where they were raised rather than at their present home in California. It was a disappointment to their families on the east coast who were looking forward to a California vacation. But having their wedding in the east, near their aging parents, helped them limit the guest list of relatives and friends to only those who lived locally. This eliminated hurting anyone's feelings since they both have large extended families throughout the United States.

It is important to invite everyone that is important to you even if you don't think they will come. Everyone likes be recognized as an important part of your life and someone with whom you want to share your special event. You will be surprised and pleased when you get a response card back from someone you had no idea would be able to attend. Everyone loves a celebration and they will endure extreme inconveniences and expense to be a part of your wedding. These are the family and friends that make up the core of your extended family and who want to be a part of your wedding. On the other hand, don't be disappointed or take it personally if someone you thought would attend declines your invitation. Today, everyone has such busy, complicated lives, and in some cases, limited financial resources. Be sensitive to the people who decline your invitation. Consider their circumstances and be sure to include them in any after-wedding correspondence you send to guests who were able to attend.

WEDDING COORDINATOR or CONSULTANT
is the Sixth Most Important Detail

Because you are getting married later in life, you may have planned a previous wedding for yourself, attended many weddings and been in many weddings. And therefore, you may think you know all about designing your own wedding. However, there are many, many more details to planning a wedding than you think, especially when it is your own. We believe you will enjoy the process more, and possibly save money, by using a wedding coordinator. This is important whether your wedding venue is in town or at a distant location. A wedding consultant is a title with the broadest definition. It has been said that the best coordinator is one who no one knows is there!

A wedding coordinator is more than a person who manages the details and the timing of your wedding ceremony. A professional wedding consultant is a person who works with you from the inception of planning your wedding to the end of the reception when the band is packing up their instruments. How much information and support you need or want will determine who you hire. Therefore, you must define your expectations and prioritize the elements of the wedding you want the coordinator to manage.

The process of finding and hiring this person will take time and is especially important for a destination or out of the country wedding. Don't even think about doing a wedding abroad without a professional consultant or a very committed friend or family member who lives in the country of your desired location. We won't get into the many complications you might face, but Marsha's daughter did get married out of the country and she could expand on this chapter for pages. The challenges her daughter faced and overcame, even with using a great wedding consultant familiar with the wedding venue, would definitely convince you to hire a wedding coordinator.

An excellent wedding consultant may cost thousands of dollars and will probably be in great demand. However, this doesn't mean this individual will be the right coordinator for you. The two of you will work very closely together, at a very emotional time of your life, so it is important for you to find someone who makes you feel comfortable and confident. It is important to interview several people to find the perfect person for you.

When interviewing the wedding consultant, these are the things you should ask or expect:

- How many other brides will they be managing when working for you?
- Will they use assistants?
- Will they personally be available the day of the wedding?
- Ask for their references and check them thoroughly.
- Ask them to identify if there is the possibility of additional add-on fees.

- Ask if they have liability insurance to cover your expenses if they are not able to deliver the services identified in their contract.
- All of the specific details you both have agreed upon should be written in the contract.
- Carefully review the contract with Mr. Wonderful before signing and giving the coordinator any money.
- Do not give the complete payment when you initiate the contract. Instead, have the coordinator produce a payment schedule that coincides when the major costs are incurred.
- Add a final payment at the end of the wedding to ensure everything went smoothly and last minute details were attended to and taken care of.

You might be able to negotiate the coordinator's basic fees. But remember, the money they will save you by helping you make the right decisions, finding the right vendors, and taking a large bit of the worrying off your shoulders, is worth all the money in the world. A respected, successful consultant knows how to interact with people in the wedding trades so they work for a fair price and don't take advantage of the situation. A wedding is expensive, and you want to have the wedding of your dreams, so hiring the right wedding coordinator will make everything easier and smoother for you and everyone else!

If you haven't budgeted for a wedding coordinator, it might be a consideration to factor in when choosing a location. Some venues staff their own coordinator. This is helpful because they understand the location and can anticipate all the problems and solutions from their prior experiences.

If you have decided against hiring a wedding consultant, identify family and friends who you would like to be involved in the planning process. Everyone loves a wedding and to be asked to participate in the planning and execution of your wedding will be received as an honor. Don't ask just one person to do all of the work, especially if you have already asked them to be in the wedding. Discuss your wedding budget with the people helping you and make it very clear you don't expect them to pay for anything. Sometimes, a person's time and commitment to help you when you need them is more valuable than anything else.

The number of people you have asked to assist with your wedding plans depends on what areas you need help with and what your budget is for the wedding. On your timeline, identify who is going to assist you with the projects with which you have asked for help. However, if you are having a local wedding, and you are familiar with the vendors, perhaps handling all the pre-wedding details will easily fit into your schedule.

If your wedding is small, asking a good friend, family member, or one of the vendors to act as a point person to coordinate all the details involved in the events of the day may be all the assistance you need. Bottom line, do not try to save money on this issue. Use a coordinator where you need one. A friend is helpful but you need someone who is objective, knows the location and vendors, and has the experience. As we mentioned earlier, we do not think it is a good idea to ask anyone involved in the wedding party to be your wedding coordinator, least of all your mother.

Whomever you select to help you manage your wedding details, make sure they understand what you want, your style and the pace you can manage. It is important when selecting an individual to make sure their organizational skills, background, creativity and personality are the right fit for you. Communicate your needs and preferences and don't feel insecure or intimidated if you change your mind several times or are unsure of what you want. Utilize the energy, commitment and expertise of everyone you have involved in your wedding but always remember this is your wedding and they must embrace your own unique style.

A church wedding often includes a wedding coordinator as a condition of using the church. You may also get lucky with the reception venue if they have their own event coordinator. Either way, we still recommend you identify a wedding consultant early in the process of planning your wedding even if you only use them on an hourly basis as an advisor. It is very helpful to have an expert give you ideas, help you identify what you need to do, the order in which you should do them, how long everything will take and how much you should budget for each item. Meet with an advisor before you make any financial commitments and sign any contracts. Using a wedding coordinator or consultant will ultimately save you time, money and additional stress.

STATIONERY
is the Seventh Most Important Detail

You have decided on the date and location of your wedding and now it is time to start making some decisions about the style you want to design your wedding around. Stationery is the perfect place to begin forming specific ideas about the look and feeling you want to create. And it will not be an expensive mistake to correct if you change your mind and want to go in another direction later. Making a decision about your stationery is an easy way to commit yourself to the process of planning your wedding.

Stationery is one of the most important and least expensive elements of your wedding style and it should match the formality of the occasion. You will be using paper products in many different ways and for a number of different reasons. Not all of the elements we will talk about in this chapter will be necessary for your particular event but we have tried to address all the possible uses for your stationery and the benefits of using each.

There are many forms of stationery to consider with your wedding and all are unique in their own purpose.

- Engagement Announcements
- Wedding Announcements
- Save the Date Cards

- Wedding Invitations
- Response Cards
- Maps or Directions
- At Home Cards
- Wedding Programs
- Place Cards
- Menu Cards
- Thank you Cards
- Personalized Note Cards
- Post Wedding Announcements

You may not need or want to purchase all of the stationery elements. This will be up to you and your own personal style.

Stationery Timeline

If possible, begin the stationery selection process three months before the actual date you want to mail your printed correspondence or as soon as you have confirmed the date and location. However, you may be like Elizabeth and not have the luxury of time to dutifully plan according to traditional guidelines…such as a year in advance. Don't dismay! The process can be sped up in many creative ways through friends, resources, an efficient stationery store or the Internet.

Create a timeline that includes each piece of correspondence you will send. Give yourself a month to research different stationery stores in your area and to decide on the style you are going to use. This style will be reflected in all the stationery items you choose. Once you have decided on your wedding invitations, it may take two to three weeks to receive the proof. After you have approved the order, it can take another two weeks to be completed and returned to you. You may be able to speed up the process if you are willing to pay a surcharge but it is better to give yourself a lot of time so your decision will not be influenced by time constraints. Once you have received the invitations, give yourself ten days to address and mail them. More time should be allowed if you want someone to personally calligraphy your envelopes or you want them hand stamped by the post office. An announcement can be sent out as soon as you are ready to announce that you are engaged. The save-the-date card should be sent out four to six months in advance of the wedding, and your wedding invitations should be sent out six weeks prior to the date of your ceremony.

Stationery Components

Start as soon as you get engaged.

- Engagement or Wedding Announcement – as soon as you are ready
- Save the Date Card – send six months to nine months before the wedding
- Website: develop six to nine months before the wedding
- Wedding Invitation – send six to eight weeks before the wedding
- Menu Cards – one month before the wedding
- Wedding Program – one month before the wedding
- Thank You Cards – as soon as possible but no later than one year after the wedding

Deciding on Your Stationery Style

Your stationery choice should complement many parts of your wedding and is a safe and simple place to imprint your style. It will not be an expensive mistake to correct if you change your mind. Stationery is a very important element and it is the first element of your wedding style that your guests will see when they receive your save the date card. For those unable to attend, your stationery is the only image they will have of your wedding. You want to immediately create an impression of your event through the style or theme you have chosen. For example, you may want to choose casual stationery for a beach wedding or more sophisticated stationery for a country club or destination wedding.

Stationery is relatively inexpensive in comparison to the other expenses associated with your wedding, but don't underestimate this item. Besides being cost effective, it can be a very creative way to define your style which will continue throughout your wedding. But remember, you will also have to take into account postage, printing and calligraphy costs!

If you decide to send out engagement announcements, start looking for stationery as soon as you can. Your first public announcement should be given serious consideration because it will be the first correspondence sent by you and Mr. Wonderful to all the people who are important to you. It is not critical to coordinate all your stationery around one style but selecting one significant theme, color or design that can be easily duplicated will make the rest of your decisions much easier. Taking the time to compile your guest list and discuss the style of your wedding early in your engagement will help you grasp the reality of the fact that you really are going to get married. It is really happening and not just a dream!

Even if the wedding date has not been firmly set, developing some opinions about your stationery will help you get organized. So when you do start preparing for the wedding, you will have already made some initial decisions between the two of you. This will begin the process of sharing mutual decisions throughout your marriage.

We recommend visiting specialty stationery stores and browse through as many sample books as you have the energy and interest to look through. Take advantage of the expertise of the employees who specialize in invitations. Describe to them what appeals to you and your image of the style in which you want to express yourself. Is your style traditional, contemporary, floral or whimsical? You will find that some designs instantly stand out while others can be easily eliminated. Spread out your selections and eliminate your least favorites. Take notes and summarize what you like. Ask the store to make a copy of your favorite selections and don't forget to inquire if there will be additional postage charges due to the size. This information may influence your decision.

If you have not found the perfect choice, go to another store. Different stores represent different stationery companies all of which present diverse ideas. Some stores carry small, unique vendors or local artists who will personalize and embellish your look whereas other stores specialize in more customary styles. Even with the more traditional designs, there are amazing computer programs that can customize a simple invitation to make a presentation that perfectly expresses the style you want to achieve.

Besides the basic design of the stationery, consider the quality and color of the paper, the font choices available, the ink color options, the style of the envelope, and the charge for any customizations. When evaluating your choices, remember there are innumerable options that can be changed and combined to get the look you want.

Your stationery can also be adapted to your budget depending on a variety of factors. Some considerations are the number of inserts such as tissue dividers or if you want the envelopes lined. All of these components can add or save on costs. The printing company and the type of printing process can also influence your decision. Expect the printer to prepare a preview sample of what you have chosen, or designed, and nothing should be ordered without your final approval.

The staff will help you understand the importance of the weight of the paper, the look of a lined envelope and the difference in printing options and costs. Afterwards, you may choose to order through them or research the Internet for a more cost-effective alternative. The time you spend in stationery stores is time well spent, especially if you decide to eventually order on-line.

The Internet vs. a Stationery Store

Prioritize which details are the most important for you to create your own style. Some advantages for using the Internet is that it can be less expensive, there are many more choices, it is easier to customize and your stationery style can be extended to your Internet bridal page.

Using a stationery store may initially take more time because you have to travel from store to store but you will get personal attention from an informed sales person who will give you advice based on their experience. They have the ability to pay attention to details you are not aware of and you can see and touch the stationery they represent. This allows you to see the paper and printing quality. Another plus is that they are responsible for any errors. Although the Internet provides a vast resource of stationery options, having a professional at the store to oversee and personally advise you on your selection may save you additional costs later on because they will guarantee accuracy and perfect printing with a timely delivery. Also, seeing and touching the paper will allow you to experience its quality and reviewing the completed invitation will give you the opportunity to confirm you have created the style you hoped to achieve.

If you decide to use the Internet, you can have the company send you a sample of each piece of stationery before you place an order, but if there are errors or you have questions, you will have to manage the process yourself. You want to feel confident with the design you created and the application of that design on the different pieces of stationery you have decided to use. When making the decision between the Internet and a stationery store, consider what is more convenient and comfortable for you. Some of us are more computer savvy than others and love the convenience of ordering over the Internet. But if you are not that person, let a professional assist you with the process of designing and ordering your stationery.

The goal is to get started with planning your wedding and we think stationery is good place to start.

One note of caution, if you do decide to order your stationery through the Internet, allow yourself more time than if you ordered directly from a store. With the Internet, your ordering procedure is different; you order samples, you decide what you want to purchase, you place your order, you receive and approve samples of what you ordered, and then you confirm your order. All of which has to be done before the stationery is submitted for production. If you were working with a retailer, they would have the exact invitation, paper samples and printing options on site. This is something to consider if your time is limited.

You may also think about designing and creating your own invitations. With the vast array of plain card stock, scrap booking, and computer design programs, you can create a look all your own. The creative, handmade touches that you put into your stationery are what will make your style unique. The addition of personalized note cards, thank you cards, place cards or a post-wedding announcement can all be a simplified version of your design.

Once you have found the invitation you want to use, consult with Mr. Wonderful. He may not like the bows or the printing style you have chosen. To be certain your fiancé feels involved and his opinion is respected, be prepared with two or three alternatives all of which you like. Don't be defensive if his choice is not your favorite, you can always compromise. Mr. Wonderful probably isn't familiar with all the different options available when choosing stationery and perhaps he has never even had a thought about what his personal style is. Remember, you are asking him to think about, and agree with you, about something out of his realm of experience. You may have to compromise which is hard since you are working through the wedding decisions based on what you like…but now is a great time to relax, meet in the middle and be creative about combining elements of both of your styles – just as you will be doing for the rest of your life. The trick is to change your attitude and learn to enjoy a new perspective while preserving your individuality.

From personal experience, Marsha's husband didn't have many opinions about the wedding until he was asked. It turned out he was very clear about wanting a formal, traditional invitation without fancy froufrou bows! Marsha wanted something a bit different so she enclosed the traditional invitation and inserts in a deep purple folder that closed uniquely and was fastened with a gold monogrammed seal embossed with their personal logo. All of which was inserted in an envelope that was lined with the same deep purple as the folder. Mike got his traditional invitation presented in less than a traditional way and they both loved the impression and style it presented.

Engagement Announcements

The way you decide to announce your engagement will probably reflect your personalities. You may want to personally contact the people who are most important to you, you may want to send out an email blast to friends and family, or you may want to send a formal announcement. Depending on your position in the community and in your work environment, you may want to inform certain people first so they are not hurt if they hear your news from another source. When Mr. Wonderful asks you to marry him, you want to shout your news from the roof tops and everyone will want to know the story of where, when and how he asked you. You will be on Cloud 9 so enjoy the attention because this time will become one of your favorite memories.

Sending a personal note is a very special way to communicate and let your friends and family know you have fallen in love and plan to marry. It will make everyone aware you have found the man of your dreams, are in a committed relationship and will soon be married. You can formally announce your engagement by sending out a simple card or a more traditional wedding announcement that follows the format of a traditional wedding invitation. This announcement can also be used as a save-the-date card if everyone you are sending it to will be invited to the wedding. Sending engagement announcements helps you to evaluate the size of your wedding and who you want to invite versus who you think may come.

After you announce your engagement, don't be surprised at all the parties people will want to plan in your honor. You may think it is insulting or not necessary for us to remind you of some basic social skills. But remember, you are combining families, different social circles and you may find yourself in situations where you know very few of the guests. They may be your future in-law's, neighbors, family you haven't met or some of your fiancé's business associates. You may be exhausted or not in the mood to meet one more new person. But whatever the occasion, it has been given in your honor and greeting your guests at the door as they arrive is important. This does not necessarily mean a formal reception line but you must give everyone a warm welcome and recognize the time they have given to come to celebrate you and Mr. Wonderful.

It is important for you both to go over the guest list before every event and be prepared with names and who is associated with whom. It is natural and comfortable to gravitate to people you know, however it is important to mingle throughout the evening and to introduce guests to each other. Even though you may not be the host or hostess, you are the reason everyone is there. These are the friends and family who will be a part of your wedding and the purpose of parties and receptions is for all these people to get to know each other and to get to know you better. These social functions are to celebrate the commitment you have both made to each other and it is up to both of you to create a level of comfort and inclusion for all those attending. New friendships and the reunion of old friends will be a major factor in the memories that everyone will associate with your marriage.

Save-the-Date Card and Enclosures

The save-the-date card provides advance notice of the date and location of your wedding which is especially helpful for people with busy schedules who need to plan ahead. It also serves many other functions and helps to keep your official wedding invitation unencumbered with inserts. Advance communication with your guests is very important, especially if you are planning a destination wedding and your guests need to make travel plans in advance.

You can also use the save-the-date card to provide transportation and hotel information as well as specific stores where you are registered for gifts. If you do not want gifts, or would prefer donations to your favorite charity in lieu of gifts, this is where you would inform your guests of this choice.

Your card can also list the activities that have been arranged around the wedding weekend with specific contact numbers if they need more information. The save-the-date card also provides a comfortable opportunity to clarify if children are invited. If they are not, list babysitting services for your guest's convenience if they want to bring their children. Also, remind them to check your wedding website frequently for any updates and provide a phone number on the card for people who do not have access to a computer.

Wedding Invitations

The wedding invitation should be specific to the ceremony. For a formal invitation, there really is no difference between a first and second wedding as the same basic rules are followed. The wording should be completely spelled out with no abbreviations. This includes names, dates, numbers, times and locations. This rule also applies to less formal invitations. The ceremony itself does not require an RSVP. However, if you are including a response card, the correct wording would be, "Kindly respond by…" or "The favor of a reply is requested by…"

If you want to send a completely informal invitation, the venue and your personalized style will dictate the wording and look of the invitations.

If your wedding is going to be very small and intimate, it is proper to send a handwritten note following the etiquette of a formal invitation or in the form of a letter.

If you are having a small, personal wedding followed by a large reception, design your invitation around the specifics of the reception and insert another, smaller card in the invitation for the guests you want to include in the official wedding ceremony.

If you have two different names, one associated with your business and another one socially, you may include both on the invitation with the less important name in parenthesis.

Elizabeth Wick James
(Elizabeth Thornton)

The wording on your wedding invitation can follow traditional, formal guidelines or you can decide on your own wording as it applies to you. If you are unsure about how to phrase the wording on your invitation, you can refer to an up-to-date etiquette book or ask the salesperson who is helping you at the stationery store for suggestions. Your decision will be made according to what is appropriate for your wedding circumstances. You can be creative with your invitation and how you word it but be sure you have included your groom in your decisions. This is especially true when the children are going to be included on the invitation. You want him to be comfortable and supportive of the choices you make. If Mr. Wonderful likes your stationery choices, he will probably love the rest of your style decisions!

If you are blending families, and want to include your children on the invitation as another way of uniting families, two suggestions are:

Elizabeth James and Stephen Berberich
Together with our children
Request the honor of your presence at
Our wedding
or
Samantha and Thomas James
and
Kathryn and Robert Berberich

Request the honor of your presence
At the marriage of their parents
Elizabeth James
and
Stephen Berberich

Response Cards

A response card is included in the invitation packet and is necessary to identify the information you need to accommodate your guest(s). It is a separate card indicating who will or will not be attending and your guests are asked to return the card by a specific date. The wording of the response card should include a place to identify how many people are responding to the card. If you have sent an invitation to a single person, and offered them the opportunity to bring a guest, the card should provide a space for that guest to be identified by name. If you are serving a formal sit down dinner and want to give your guests a choice of entrees, include this information on the card as well as a space to indicate if they have any food allergies. Be sure to enclose a stamped, return envelope. Your guests will appreciate the stamp and you will have a better chance of getting the card returned in a timely manner.

You have a lot of wedding details to handle so consider having someone else be responsible for receiving and managing the response cards. Unfortunately, there will be some people who will not return their cards on time and it is an awkward and time consuming task to personally contact them to get the information you need. So, let someone else do it. You may want to do everything yourself, but try to delegate as much as you can. That is why you have attendants.

Maps and Directions

Small maps and directions should also be included in your invitation packet as well as available on your website.

Post Wedding Announcements

A wedding announcement sent after the ceremony is appropriate if you are having a small, private ceremony or you made a spontaneous decision to get married and elope. There are circumstances when couples who have had a large wedding send announcements to uninvited friends and family, but this announcement should be carefully worded. You don't want to unintentionally hurt someone's feelings who wasn't invited to the wedding, and you don't want your announcement to be interpreted as a "gift" announcement. If you don't want the announcement to elicit a gift response, clearly indicate no gifts are expected.

At Home Cards

A nice addition to include in any of your correspondence before or after the wedding is an "At Home Card" with the address of your residence, phone numbers, email addresses, as well as your new married name. This information should also be available on your website.

It is important for a newly married woman to inform everyone of the name she has chosen to use after the wedding. It will eliminate a lot of confusion and unnecessary explanations if everyone is aware of how you want to be addressed as a married woman. As a modern, mature bride, the name you take at this time of your life is an important decision and one we cover more thoroughly in another chapter.

Envelopes

Don't forget to include the envelope as an important part of the presentation of your style. The envelope is the first thing that is seen by the recipient and should be included in the total look or theme of your stationery. A traditional invitation is usually sent with a lined envelope. However, invitations are now being sent in all kinds of creative envelopes and containers.

Be sensitive to color so the address can be clearly read by the postal scanning equipment and the delivery person. Also, be aware of the postal requirements for weight and size. Take your completed invitation to the post office to have it weighed before adding your stamps.

After you have made your envelope choice, decide if you want the envelopes personally addressed by a calligrapher, a stationery store with a calligraphy machine, or a dear friend with beautiful handwriting. Add an additional two weeks to accomplish this task. Adding an embossed stamp with your logo or combined initials is a nice touch and you can use the personalized embosser for years to come. You can get fancy and use a wax stamp or make it easy and use a personalized label to finish sealing the envelope.

When ordering, add 20% more envelopes than you think is necessary because you will need them if you make an error in writing an address. If you are using a computer to address the envelopes, they may jam in the printing process or you might need to resend an invitation because the original was returned.

Stamps

A nice touch that adds to your style without deducting too much from your pocketbook is personalized stamps. If you have time and can afford the additional expense, create your own stamp with your own design or picture. Stamps.com is one site that will create almost any design you can think of.

The US Postal Service usually has stamps with a wedding theme, but they can be seasonal and are not always available. Visit their website at www.usps.com as there is a wider selection that is not always available at your local post office and they can be ordered directly online. Also be aware of postal regulations. Both the size and the weight of your complete invitation will determine the cost of the mailing. Square envelopes and some small envelopes incur a higher mailing cost because they do not meet the standard postal regulations. Check in your area to see if your post office offers hand stamping of envelopes which will eliminate any lines that will distract from the presentation of your invitation. This is always a nice touch and will show your attention to details which is part of your style

The Wedding Program

You may or may not feel it is important to present your guests with a program for your ceremony. This decision may be dictated by the size and location of the wedding, the number of people in the wedding party, the religious denomination if you are getting married in a church or if you are having a long service with many songs and readings.

A wedding program gives your guests something to look at while they are waiting for the wedding to start and gives them some personal information about who is in the wedding and why they are important to you. It is a nice place to identify and honor immediate family members who have passed away and it provides the bride and groom with another opportunity to thank everyone for their attendance. It is also the place to inform your guests if there are any house standards they should be aware of.

A program is essential if you want guest participation in any part of the service and it is the perfect place to put the the details of, and directions to, the the reception. Your guests will especially appreciate this detail if they have forgotten to bring their original invitation with the map. You may also add your new address, phone numbers, email addresses and any other information you have on your At Home Card.

Creating a wedding program is simple because it will be designed around your wedding style with all the elements of the ceremony titled and listed according to the order of their performance. The usher usually hands the programs to each guest but they can also be placed on the chairs beforehand or offered on a centrally located table.

Don't forget to put this item on your time line because it is one of those details that is easily forgotten until the last minute!

Place Cards and Seating Arrangements

Seating arrangement boards and place cards are the easiest way to direct your guests to their table and there are many creative ways to give them this information. The first and most casual way is to display a seating chart which identifies the table where each guest is to sit. Or the preferred way is to have a table at the entrance to the reception with each guest's name on a card noting their table number. Couples will only need one card. When your guest has responded they will be bringing another person, be sure to find out that person's name because everyone should have their own name displayed. Using place cards on the table eliminates any confusion as to where each person should sit and also helps everyone know who is at their table. You can also use the place card as a thank you note expressing how much you appreciate their attendance.

There is an unlimited number of ways to express your style by how you display the table cards. You can make the place cards part of the table decoration by using small picture frames, display the cards as part of your floral theme, or even going so far as placing a picture of each person on the place card instead of their name! Time will only limit your creativity and ideas.

Menu Cards

Personalized menu cards offer another opportunity to display your wedding theme but they are not necessary and may be one detail you can leave out. If you want a menu card, some caterers will offer one at no charge. One suggestion is to have a menu creatively displayed in a picture frame on the table where your guests pick up their place card. Or there can be a menu on each table that can be passed around if anyone is interested. Besides tempting your guests with the fabulous dinner they will be enjoying, it is important to have a menu available to inform guests of their dinner options in case they might have a food allergy.

Personalized Stationery

We have been told that ordering personalized stationery, with your married name, before the wedding brings bad luck. If you are not superstitious, don't worry. An option is to use your first names or initials on a note card that reflects your wedding style and wait to order personalized stationery with your new name and/or initials after your honeymoon.

Thank You Cards

Customized thank you cards, designed in the same style as your stationery, are an important detail that ties your entire engagement and wedding together. The card can be blank for you to write a personal message to each of your guests or it can be printed with a message that can be individualized with a brief note.

Many people come to weddings with their cameras, but they forget to take pictures of themselves. During your reception, arrange for candid pictures to be taken of everyone and include them in your thank-you notes. If you plan to send pictures, remember to order cards with envelopes that will accommodate the standard 4"x 6" picture size.

You can also make a memorable thank you card by creating a postcard. Friends and family leave a wedding with great mental images but very few of them get to see the wedding pictures. Now, with digital imaging, your wedding pictures are available almost immediately and can be used in a number of ways to commemorate the day. Picture collages of some of the memorable moments of the wedding make a great postcard to send to your guests as one last thank you for sharing your day. And for those of us that are not good at writing thank you notes, a postcard is also nice because it limits the length of the note you have to write. Grooms love them!

WEBSITE
is the Eighth Most Important Detail

Most of your friends and family actively communicate with each other on the Internet so use this convenience to share the details of your wedding plans with them. Using the Internet to communicate with your guests is a very simple, quick and less formal way to provide information on a variety of topics. It is easy to develop a web page through bridal websites like "The Knot" or you can create one on your own. A website helps to give specific details and information about your wedding that otherwise would clutter up the simplicity of your beautiful invitation. Create an email directory of your guests when you are compiling your guest list. A good way to let your guests know about your site is to send them an email announcing your engagement at which time you invite them to periodically visit your site to keep informed as your wedding plans develop.

A website should not replace your save-the-date card or wedding invitation, but it is an effective way to communicate to your guests about any changes that may come up after the save-the-date or wedding invitations have been sent. Your website will provide a convenient way to make information available about transportation, hotels, babysitters, additional wedding weekend events and other pertinent information as well as provide a link to your gift registry. Some guests may even use your site as a portal to talk to one another about plane fares, who will be arriving and when, hotel or home rentals and any other important information.

It is a quick, easy and convenient way to convey all your wedding plans, it facilitates your guests communicating directly with you and helps you address questions that are specific to their needs. All of which eliminates a lot of last minute confusion and concerns.

Keep in mind that not everyone is computer savvy or familiar with the Internet. If some details of your wedding are not included in your announcement or invitation, be sure to follow-up with a phone call to your guests who are not active on the Internet.

CEREMONY
is the Ninth Most Important Detail

The wedding ceremony and reception are two separate components of planning a wedding. They can be planned together or individually depending on the situation and you will need a separate budget for each. Traditionally, they have always been planned together. If you do not want a traditional wedding, there are as many ways to plan your wedding as you have the imagination to create. There are many factors that will help with this decision. The choices may vary from having your wedding and reception at the same location, having your wedding at one location followed by a reception at another location, deciding to have a small wedding and no reception, having a reception at a later date, or having several receptions. Marrying at this time of your life may open up interesting options that you would not have considered at another time of your life.

The Wedding Ceremony

The purpose of the wedding ceremony is to commemorate and rejoice in the commitment you have made to each other. It is a solemn ritual that is a legally important contract and often a religious sacrament. Invite all your close family and friends to the ceremony and surround yourself with people who love you. As you start to plan your service, consider any specific religious readings, special poems, music or songs you would like to include in your ceremony. Think about any special remembrances or touches you want to include to make this unforgettable occasion one of the best memories of your life.

You certainly don't need to follow all of the conventional wedding traditions. Only do what has significance for you and Mr. Wonderful. One of the marvelous aspects of being a modern, mature bride is you can disregard any tradition that does not have a special meaning for you. Use your imagination to create your own personal wedding experience. If you have always wanted a big wedding with all the trimmings, which might not have been possible in your first marriage or when you were younger, then go for it!

Religious Ceremony

When you get married in a church, there will be many rules to follow depending on the doctrines of the religion. Sometimes these rules can be changed and other times they must be strictly adhered to. Adding your own vows, or some personal musical selections, are often changes that must be approved by the church. There may be additional guidelines that you and your guests must follow such as women covering their heads or the prohibiting of flash photography. It is important to add this information to your invitation and website. Alert your ushers to these rules. You can also place a sign outside the church reminding you guests of these requirements, and if necessary, have scarves available for women who need to be covered.

Interfaith Ceremony

When both of you are of different faiths, you may choose to combine traditions and have a separate Officiate present for each religion. This situation is not as unusual as it use to be because the world is quickly changing and there is more integration between cultures and races. Intertwining the rituals and symbolism of each other's faith will add a personal touch to your ceremony. It is helpful and appreciated by your guests if you provide an explanation in your wedding program of the traditions you are including in your wedding service. This way they can follow along and understand the significance of the rituals they are witnessing.

Some faiths are very strict about their religious traditions and will not allow their clerics to perform a ceremony within their church walls that includes an official from another belief. However, the Catholic Church has revised their policy and Priests can take part in mixed marriages and co-preside at wedding in Churches other than Catholic ones. Now they can give a blessing after the other Officiate has pronounced the Bride and Groom "man and wife." But they cannot perform the actually marriage ceremony and or do the pronouncing. When faced with these challenges, you will both have to make a compromise. You might be able to get married in a church that is more flexible and incorporate the religious traditions that are most meaningful to each you. Another alternative is to find an interfaith, or non-denominational minister, who will be willing to accommodate the religious traditions of both of your faiths. When you do find this individual, it is important to meet several times so they understand the significant and personal elements you want them to include in your wedding to ensure a service that is a meaningful ceremony for each of you.

Civil Ceremony

A civil ceremony is a simple and expedient way to get married. A mayor, judge or any legally qualified Officiate can usually perform a legal marriage ceremony in a public or government office. A justice of the peace, or an individual licensed by the state, is also qualified to administer your wedding vows.

A civil ceremony commonly follows a basic script although sometimes you may be able to personalize it. Musical elements and other normal wedding touches are usually not allowed. It is a very basic ceremony that is designed to make your marriage legal. You must have two witnesses in attendance to sign your certificate and you may include a few guests to watch the ceremony. Unlike traditional church or venue weddings, there is no fluff, only the basics! Civil ceremonies allow you to get married without the stress and expense of a large wedding. If you want to celebrate the event with friends and family after the ceremony, you can include them in a dinner or reception.

Secular Ceremony

Secular ceremonies take place at a location that is not a consecrated church such as a country club, restaurant, resort, hotel, beach, private home or any other location you choose to be married. Depending on the rules of your church, your priest or minister may or may not be allowed to perform your wedding ceremony outside the auspices of their church and you will have to locate an independent Officiate who is willing to perform a ceremony that includes your personal religious beliefs. Although a secular ceremony can include many religious elements such as readings from the Bible, religious songs and some religious traditions, the overall ceremony is not religious. Therefore, it will be up to you and Mr. Wonderful to determine the tone and style of your wedding ceremony.

Writing Your Vows

Your vows not only show true commitment to your beloved partner but they also express your understanding of the responsibilities of marriage you are assuming with the promise you are making.

Writing and delivering your personal vows and declaration of love to each other may seem very romantic in the planning phase. But remember, you are probably going to be very emotional at the time of the ceremony which will make it difficult for you to speak loudly and clearly. Even if you are a competent speaker, your professional self may be thrown off guard with the emotions of the moment. Make sure your wedding Officiate has a copy of what you plan to say to each other so they can prompt you if it becomes necessary. Be certain both you and the Officiate use a microphone and practice using it at the rehearsal. This is not the time to be shy but don't over estimate your composure. Nerves can make your voice change and divert your attention. The Officiate is there to perform a function both legal and emotional so look to him/her for support and timing. Don't count on your groom because he will probably be more overwhelmed with the moment than you are!

For the ceremony, decide if you will recite traditional vows or write your own. Your vows may be completely untraditional unless this is not sanctioned by your church, or you may only want to modify the traditional language of your vows for the exchange of your rings. You can also ask your friends and family to participate in some portion of your wedding vows.

If you choose to create your own vows, the Internet is a great resource. You can use the Internet to review the wording of a traditional wedding service or get advice on how to write your vows "in six easy steps"! You will find an incredible number of subject titles to search. We even found interesting ideas under obscure subjects such as "lawful wedded wife", "days of our life" and "generous person".

Some couples write funny vows. However, use caution when diverging too far from the concept and language of traditional vows. Keep your vows personal and make sure they reflect who you are as a person and what you are promising as a lifetime partner.

Before your witnesses, you are both making a solemn promise you will stay together in all circumstances: whether happy or sad and through good or bad times. In a very profound way, your vows express that you will be there for each other forever. By keeping these vows alive in your marriage, they will give you both comfort, they will confirm your commitment to each other and you will always feel secure in your marriage.

Additional Elements to the Wedding Ceremony

Candle lighting, or a "Unity Candle Ceremony", can be included as part of your religious ceremony representing a symbolic moment when your guests take time to pray, reflect and remember. The lighting can be used to symbolize bringing families together or to remember family members who have passed away. It is also provides an opportunity to involve other family members or close friends in your wedding.

Another modern way to celebrate family unity, or provide a thoughtful moment to remember people who can't be with you on this day, is to perform a Unity Sand Ceremony. This is also a great way to get around the use of candles if they are impractical or not allowed, especially if your wedding is on the beach or at a windy location. In this new tradition, you and Mr. Wonderful each have your own vase filed with different colored sand. As you recite your vows, you each exchange pouring your sand into one vase. Near the end of your vows, you pour the remainder of your sand together, signaling your union of marriage. Your Sand Vase will then become another memorable keepsake of your ceremony.

Seating

It is customary and a tradition to seat the bride's guests on the left and groom's guests on the right. Today, people are not usually as concerned with where they sit during the ceremony as they use to be. Some wedding coordinators like to have the bride's family sit on the right so they can look at her during the ceremony, but this is not traditional and can be confusing for you and your guests. If you change the tradition of the groom's friends and family on the right and bride's family and friends on the left, make sure your ushers are prepared to direct the guests and provide an explanation. Ushers are a nice touch to your wedding ceremony. They not only greet your guests but also help seat them in an orderly fashion.

A wedding is not a popularity contest, but it is better to have the guests evenly placed to ensure that one side is not more populated than the other. If your wedding ceremony is not at a traditionally venue, ushers are necessary to explain where the guest should go, identify and provide chairs for the people that may not be able to stand for a long period, and be the eyes and ears for the wedding party so they know when the guests are seated and the wedding can begin.

A church wedding dictates where you should sit, but a non-church wedding offers different opportunities for how and where to place your guests. When deciding on where you are going to seat everyone, it is important to remember you are trying to create a feeling of unity among the guests and between the families. You will want to create an atmosphere of joy and intimacy, making sure everyone can see and are comfortable. If you choose a location where everyone is expected to stand, arrange for a few chairs to be placed in a convenient location for the guests who are elderly or have limitations. Remember to keep this in mind, especially for destination or beach weddings. Standing in the sand, while waiting for you to appear gorgeous and ready to walk down the aisle, may take longer than you anticipated.

If your wedding is in the afternoon or early evening, seat your guests so the sun is not directly in their eyes. It is thoughtful to provide an awning, sun umbrellas or a pair of fun sunglasses for those who come unprepared.

Other Details

Be creative and don't be afraid to customize or personalize anything and everything to establish and enhance your wedding theme and make your wedding event memorable for you and all your guests. To add variety and a touch of unity to the ceremony, you may want to have the signing of the marriage certificate included as part of the ceremony. However, traditionally this is done after the wedding with selected members of your wedding party who are required to sign the certificate as your witnesses. Besides the usual music, prayers, readings, candle lighting and vows, feel free to include anything else that is important to both of you. Marsha got married on a golf course green, and since both her and Mike's deceased fathers were avid golfers, she had one of her sons and one of Mike's daughters drive a golf ball in their fathers' honor. Jennifer out drove Ben, but he said he shanked the ball just like his grandfather usually did from the first tee. It truly added a touch of celebration and honor to the ceremony.

Remember that honoring tradition is wonderful, but you are a mature modern bride and have the personal freedom to integrate your ideas with the traditional wedding elements to create a memory that you will reflect on and enjoy the rest of your life.

Music

Music is an important element to your wedding ceremony and is easy to incorporate into your style. However, the type of music you choose, and how it is performed, will vary according to your ceremony's location. Traditional, classical music is usually preferred if you are to be married in a church or a secular venue. Your favorite songs that you share together should be saved for the reception. However, for a less formal, nontraditional wedding ceremony, a favorite romantic song would be a memorable touch. At a religious ceremony, an organist, singer, choral group, cantor, harpist or other singular instrument is preferred.

If you have chosen songs to be performed during the ceremony, keep them short. You'll appreciate this recommendation when you are standing at the altar looking at each other while the song is being performed. A three-minute song may seem like an eternity!

For your reception, the sky is the limit when selecting your music. The size and formality of the venue will often determine your choice. From a DJ, pre-recorded music, a singer, small band or orchestra, each type will set a different mood. You can also choose to include different styles of music at various times during the reception. As an example, you can begin the evening with a harpist who can provide background music during the pre-dinner reception and dinner, followed by a live band or rocking DJ for the dancing portion of the evening. Your entertainment can also include family members who want to participate.

Music is a part of all of our lives, however it is more important to some people than others. Some people have very specific tastes and know which type of music they like and which songs they want to hear. If you are not this person, you need to do some research and ask for recommendations from your friends. Let your wedding coordinator help you in this area and talk to vendors and other people who are familiar with your reception venue. When you have identified the performers, take the time to interview them and listen to their music to be certain they will be providing the type of music you like. Request a copy of their CD if they have one and/or a schedule of their appearances so you and Mr. Wonderful can go and listen to them in person.

When selecting your musician ask the following questions before signing a contract.

- How long will they be able to perform during your event?
- Will there be an overtime charge if you extend beyond their time limit? If so, how much?
- How many breaks will they take during the reception?
- Do they expect beverages and dinner?

Prepare a list of the songs you would like them to play, the timing of announcements you would like them to make, specific dances they should be prepared for and other events they will be participating in during the evening. The music you provide, and the personality of the DJ or band leader, is an integral part of the success of turning your reception into a party as the event progresses. If you expect the musicians to perform over several hours, you should be prepared to provide them with food and refreshments. If this is not in your budget, it is courteous to let them know ahead of time if you will not be offering them a meal.

If music is important, make it a key factor in choosing your location. Some venues have specific music requirements, limitations and time restrictions. And most locations will dictate the type of amplification.

Ways to save the dollars:
1. Use pre-recorded music for the background.
2. Hire a local high school quartet or someone from your church.

OFFICIATE
is the Tenth Most Important Detail

The individual who serves as your Officiate will depend on your religious affiliation and the location of your ceremony. If combining religious backgrounds, you may consider having a representative from both your religious affiliations participate in delivering your wedding vows. You can decide who you would like to perform the ceremony and you can add or customize almost any element of the wedding ceremony that is appropriate and important to you. You can get married in a church or have a civil ceremony. If you and your fiancé are from different religions, and you want to be married by a representative of your respective religions, it is usually easier for the clerics to participate together outside a traditional religious venue. If you choose a destination wedding, this may be harder to arrange unless you have a close personal tie with your cleric and they are willing to travel to be with you. If that is the case, it is usually customary to provide them with transportation and lodging. However, you may find it necessary, more convenient or cost effective to find someone locally. If you need to find a local Officiate, it is important you identify and meet with that person well in advance of your wedding to be certain they are the right choice. The person who performs your ceremony not only marries you by the legal definition but they also participate in one of the most important events in your life.

You should try to meet with your Officiate as many times as it is necessary for him to have an understanding of who you are individually and as a couple. It is a very emotional event and you want your Officiate to deliver a message that is both relevant and meaningful for you and your guests. If time or distance is a problem, arrange to have your meetings by phone. It is very important for your Officiate to deliver a personal message. This can only be accomplished if you both have taken the time to get to know the Officiate who is performing the ceremony and have shared with him your ideas, thoughts, concerns and insights as to why you are getting married.

Despite popular beliefs, weddings do not have to be performed by an ordained priest or minister. In fact, it is becoming a common trend to have an Officiate deliver your wedding vows. You can now have anyone preside over your wedding if they are willing to go on the Internet and fill out an application with the Universal Church of Life. There is no cost unless you request a certificate to verify they are the official minister of this church. Using a friend or family member to be your Officiate may seem sentimental, convenient or fun, but choose this person wisely. Getting married is a very serious ceremony of commitment and the Officiate must be an individual who understands and respects the position you have asked him to assume and is aware they will be performing a legal wedding ceremony, not a comedy routine. If your Officiate is not prepared, or does not take their position seriously, your wedding ceremony, including your vows, will come across to you and your guests as lacking sincerity.

If you do not know an Officiate who is familiar with you or your family, and you choose someone because they were recommended or you found him on the Internet, you will run the risk of the Officiate not being capable or sincere. There are a lot of wedding details needing your attention. It is critical and worth the time to find the right Officiate who will perform a marriage ceremony you and Mr. Wonderful are confident was written and delivered with the sensitivity and declaration of love your marriage deserves.

A question always asked is how much to pay the Officiate. If it is a small ceremony, the usual amount is $150.00. If yours is a larger, more elaborate wedding, then $200-300 is an appropriate amount. It is also thoughtful to invite the Officiate to your reception, as well as to pay for all of their travel expenses. Unless the Officiate requests otherwise, the check for his services should be made out to him personally.

Wedding Quiz for Couples

- Who do you want to Officiate your marriage?
- What kind of a wedding ceremony do you want?
- What wedding traditions are important to you?

RECEPTION
is the Eleventh Most Important Detail

Your reception will be the party that culminates and celebrates the completion of the personal, legal and religious components of your marriage, and it will be the first time you will be entertaining as a married couple.

You may have one style for your wedding and another style for your reception. You may even wear a different dress. You may invite more people to your reception than to your wedding or you may want to transition from a traditional ceremony to a flamboyant themed reception. It may even make sense for you to have it at another time of the day if your location, or number of guests, make this more convenient. Evaluate your circumstances and be creative. This is your wedding and the time to implement your fantasies of a fabulous party celebrating one of the most important days of your life!

There are no hard and fast rules about who hosts the reception. The wording on your invitation only identifies who is giving the wedding. Information regarding the reception can be included on the invitation or on a separate enclosure card. When someone hosts the reception other than the party (parties) identified on the wedding invitation, this should be conveyed in the wording on the enclosure card. If you are having a private ceremony followed by a public reception, send a formal invitation for the reception that clearly states it is only for the reception.

There are no steadfast guidelines for creating your reception, the number of receptions you have, the style you choose or the size and location. Most likely your decisions will be influenced by where the ceremony will take place. A reception traditionally follows the wedding. But if you eloped or had a destination wedding that did not include a large guest list, you may want to have a reception after your honeymoon.

If you are both originally from different parts of the country, and your family and friends cannot afford or have the time to travel, one solution might be to have two smaller receptions in different locations. These receptions needn't be overly expensive but smaller and more intimate parties to accommodate each situation. Whether they are formal dinners, cocktail parties or backyard barbeques, it is a great way for people, who might otherwise not have the opportunity to be with you, recognize and celebrate your marriage.

Prepare a list of all the elements of a traditional reception and decide what you do and do not want to do. Show your list to Mr. Wonderful to see if he has any suggestions, requests or concerns. Talk about your budget and decide how much money you want to spend in each area. As a modern mature bride, deciding who pays for the wedding and reception may be different if you have been married before, if your parents have passed away, or if other members of you or your fiancé's family have expressed an interest in being financially involved. If someone else is financially contributing to your wedding, decide at the beginning of the process if you are going to allow them to make any decisions and what aspects of your wedding you are willing to compromise on before accepting their generous offer. This is your wedding, you have determined your style and the direction of events, and you must be comfortable with all of the details and decisions that you and your fiancé have made. If someone is helping contribute to the cost of your wedding, your plans may be complicated if they think their financial contribution entitles them to control some of your decisions. It is a delicate subject and one you should be prepared to address if the situation presents itself. Many times, issues that involve money take time to sort out between everyone involved. At the end of the day, be prepared for the expenses to fall on the two of you.

In the order of where to spend the dollars, focus your budget on the wedding event. Friends or family usually give the engagement party. The family of the groom customarily hosts the rehearsal dinner and/or pre-wedding reception, and the wedding reception is usually the responsibility of the bride's family. However, you and your groom may feel more comfortable hosting the reception as a gift to your family and friends who have supported you through thick and thin and have now come to celebrate you both on your wedding day.

There are some traditional formalities to a wedding reception and you may want to include your children and other family members in these traditions. If your parents are still alive and married for many years, consider having them cut the cake and feed it to you for good luck. How symbolic and special for all four of you! If your new family includes children, another special and different twist would be to cut the cake and feed it to them. As you begin the blending of families, anything you can do to make your children feel a part of your new union will be helpful and create new memories for them.

Your reception can be many things but it is usually planned around a stand-up, casual reception and buffet, food stations or sit-down meal. Your location, time of the year, time of the day and your budget will influence this decision. The following are some things to consider when making this decision.

Questions to ask:
- Can you have a tasting day during which you get to sample of all the foods?
- Will they handle the valet parking and if so how much will that cost?
- Will they provide a printed menu?
- Will they provide a wedding cake? What will be the cutting cost per piece?
- What are their cancellation fees? If so, what is the last date you may cancel on?
- What is the deadline for a guest count?

Beverages
What liquid refreshments you serve at your reception is determined by the location, time of day and your own personal customs and preferences.

The beverages you select will determine if you need a bar and bartenders or servers. It will also determine the type of glassware you will need and how much you should have available.

Some decisions to make:

- Are you going to serve liquor and are you going to have an open bar?
- Are you going to limit your refreshments to wine, water and soft drinks?
- Will there be a champagne toast during the festivities?

Questions to ask:

- Do they have different bar packages?
- Can we bring in our own liquor? Wine? Champagne?
- How are drinks charged? By the bottle or glass?
- Is there an additional charge to pour the champagne for the wedding toast?

Ways to Save the Dollars:

- Ask if you can bring in your own wine and liquor?
- Purchase your liquor from a store that allows you to return any unopened bottles.
- Serve a domestic sparkling wine instead of champagne.
- Serve only wine, beer, water and soft drinks.
- Serve wine, beer, water, soft drinks and one signature, specialty cocktail.
- Use small wine glasses and the same size wine glass for all the different wine varieties you serve.
- Limit the wine choices to one white and one red selection
- Serve an open bar during the cocktail hour and only wine with dinner.

You can save money with the ceremonial wedding toast by not pouring a separate glass of champagne for each guest. Many guests don't like champagne or they may only accept a glass because they want to participate in the toast but only take a sip. You can always provide champagne at the bar for those who prefer it. A ceremonial toast is suggested for a formal, seated reception but it is not necessary for an informal standing reception. But if the traditional champagne toast is important to you, arrange to have poured champagne circulated on trays or rent a champagne fountain and invite everyone to help themselves.

To determine the amount of liquor you need to buy, most caterers estimate about 1 drink per person per hour. A bottle of champagne or wine contains 4-5 drinks. A bottle of liquor with a mixer will make 8-9 drinks. Mixers include club soda, tonic, soda, fruit juice, etc., and will average three containers per bottle of liquor. You have to adjust these figures by your location, the weather, the time of day and the age of your guests.

Warm weather weddings usually call for more clear liquors to add to juices and tonics. For cocktail parties, martinis are a favorite, and sit down dinners require plenty of wine. A minimum of one bottle of red and one bottle of white wine are the recommended amounts for each table. Offering a specialty signature cocktail for the evening is a cash saving tip and will be a unique statement to extend your wedding style. The drinks can be premixed ahead of time then poured into glasses and served on trays.

For a three to four hour evening reception, we recommend the following amounts. This is just a general guideline and you do not have to provide all of these choices. You know your family and friends so add that information into your equation.

A Full Bar for	100 guests	150 Guests
Red Wine	12 bottles	18 bottles
White Wine	12 bottles	18 bottles
Champagne	20 bottles	30 bottles
Beer	60 bottles	180 bottles
Vodka	2 bottles	5 bottles
Gin	2 bottles	3 bottles
Rum	2 bottles	3 bottles
Bourbon	2 bottles	4 bottles
Scotch	2 bottles	3 bottles
Tequila	1 bottle	2 bottles

A Wine & Beer	100 guests:	150 Guests
Beer	200 bottles	300 bottles
Champagne	30 bottles	45 bottles
Red Wine	36 bottles	53 bottles
White Wine	36 bottles	53 bottles

A Stand-Up Reception

A stand-up reception is more casual, doesn't last as long, is less expensive and is usually limited to serving beverages and appetizers. The food can be presented on one central table, several tables throughout the venue, or passed by servers. Besides being more informal, this type of reception will also eliminate some of your expenses such as some rental items, floral centerpieces and many other costs associated with seating everyone and serving a meal.

This social environment will also allow your guests to visit with a number of different guests and provides a comfortable way to introduce people to each other. However, this informal style does make it difficult to hold a purse, a drink, gracefully eat an appetizer, and be socially attentive without spilling or dropping something!

If you are going to have a stand-up reception, create some seating areas that provide guests a place to put their plates and glasses down so they can sit and visit with their friends. The addition of small tables throughout the venue will give people a place to congregate and allow weary or elderly guests a place to rest.

A stand-up reception does give the bride and groom the opportunity to circulate easily among their guests but this type of reception might keep you from being the center of attention. On the other hand, it might give some of your guests the opportunity to dominate your attention. Be sensitive and aware of your responsibility to circulate and visit with all your guests and make a point of visiting everyone politely excusing yourself if someone wants to monopolize your time as you move from group to group. Be conscious that some people may not feel as included in this informal setting if they do not know many other guests. This can be resolved by designating several outgoing friends or family members the responsibility of circulating and informally introducing people.

A Sit Down Reception

A sit down reception is much more involved, extends over a longer time and will be a more expensive event because you will be serving a meal.

Food

When planning your sit down reception, you have to decide what kind of food you are going to serve and how you are going to serve it. Some of your considerations include:

- Heavy appetizers
- Food Stations
- Buffet
- Casual Barbeque
- Sit Down Dinner

When planning the food menu, take into consideration your guests unique dietary requirements, food allergies, and personal preferences such as vegetarianism. If you do not have a menu planned to accommodate individual variations, ask your caterer how they manage and are prepared for guests with specific food requests. If this is part of their service, be sure to verify this has been factored in the estimate they have prepared for you. It is appropriate to ask your guests to respond to this question on their response card and put this inquiry on your wedding website.

Your location may determine the kind of food you will serve and the manner in which it will be presented to your guests. Depending on the venue and the services they can provide, you may have to look to an off-site caterer to address your needs. If your reception site is not associated with a restaurant, ask them for recommendations or get referrals from your wedding coordinator as well as from friends, recent brides or other people who might have some experience with caterers in the area.

The price of a caterer is determined by many factors, such as the time of day, number of people and how you would like the food served.

Questions to ask caterers:

- Do they offer a wedding package and if so what does it include and cost?
- What is the differential cost for sit down dinner, buffet or food stations?
- Do they provide the glassware, tableware and table coverings?
- Do you have to use their favorite vendors?
- How many servers will they provide?
- How many hours are included in their catering package and what are their overtime costs?
- If the servers must be paid separately, what are their hourly wages?
- What food and drinks will be served during the cocktail hour and later in the reception?
- Are gratuities and taxes included?

- Are there any set up fees of additional equipment rentals you should be aware of?

Seating

Whether it be a casual buffet or formal sit down dinner party, it is important to have tables assigned so guests are not confused as to where they should sit or feel awkward if they don't know many of the other guests. Place cards are extremely important to avoid any confusion with your guests.

With a large formal reception, there is usually a special table set for just for you and Mr. Wonderful. Depending on your style, you can either choose to sit at a Sweetheart Table for two, a table for four to include your Maid of Honor and Best Man, or you may want to sit with your entire wedding party or family. The age of your children will determine if it is appropriate or convenient for them to be included.

Whether your parents are divorced or not, seating at your reception should not pose a problem. If your parents are still alive and together, they should have their own table with close family and friends. Mr. Wonderful's parents should do the same. If you have siblings, it would be nice for each of them to host additional family, friends and guests who do not know many people at the wedding.

When everyone is seated, visit all the tables and say a few words to each of your guests. If there are children, the decision to seat them with other guests or create a children's table may depend on their age. If you have a separate table for the children, be sure to seat their parents nearby so they can monitor their child's behavior and possibly help them with their meal. Offering a special kids menu, as well as games or other table activities to entertain them, will be a blessing for the parents and your other guests.

Cake

Serving a custom wedding cake is very expensive because you usually pay one charge for the cake and another charge, by the slice, to have it served.

It is traditional to serve a cake, but besides being expensive, there are many people who accept a piece of cake to be polite but do not eat it. An alternative would be to have a small wedding cake for the traditional "cake cutting" pictures and then have large sheet cakes cut and personally served or put on a dessert table for your guests to serve themselves. Cupcakes are also popular, decorative and fun to eat – and they limit the calories and waste because they are small.

If the cake ceremony is important to you, consider cutting the cake and taking the pictures earlier in the reception/dinner program. Most weddings extend over hours, and if the cake is cut later in the program, many of the guests have had to leave and don't get to enjoy watching you cut and feed the cake to each other. Some brides want it all and plan a dessert course with the meal and the wedding cake as an option later in the event.

Ways to Save the Dollars:

Buy your cake from a local vendor such as a grocery store or culinary school.

Have a smaller 2-tiered cake and then matching cupcakes as additional treats.

Serve something completely out of the box such as, "do it yourself" ice cream sundaes, chocolate fountains or another dessert that is unique for your venue or evokes special memories. A friend chose strawberry shortcake as her family were strawberry farmers. Another bride, who had an outdoor wedding, chose "make your own Smores" over a wood fired pit.

Table Favors

As a modern mature bride, you are creating the wedding you want at this stage of your life and you will not be required to do anything that is traditionally expected which includes providing a favor. If you have the time, money and creativity, make the favor you select be reflective of your wedding theme and style. Personalizing them is a special touch. You can make the favor a creative place card or something they can eat or drink such as candy, cookies or wine. You can use favors to decorate the table like a customized wine glass or bud vase. The favor could even be part of the table centerpiece. The Internet is a great place to resource and find ideas.

Table favors are not expected but they offer a nice, personal touch. However, they may be difficult to present on the table with all of the dinnerware and flowers. Many people forget to take their favors home and they do add considerable cost. If you feel you would like to offer your guests an extension of your appreciation with something other than a gift, presenting them with a poem or personal note would add a special touch. Your appreciation can also be expressed in a thank you note sent after the wedding in which you could include a picture of them taken during the event.

If you are planning on a small wedding, or choose not to include table favors for your guests, a small donation to a favorite charity in their name is a nice token of your gratitude for their attendance. You can note this in your wedding program, on their place card or on your website.

PHOTOGRAPHY
is the Twelfth Most Important Detail

Based on your budget and future plans for your pictures, you have to make a decision on what type of pictures you want for your memories.

- Do you want still photos for an album?

- Do you want pictures to hang on the wall?
- Do you want slides to display on a small viewing screen?
- Do you want the pictures to be in color, black and white, sepia or a mixture of both?

When selecting a photographer, carefully review their resume, references, sample-wedding portfolio and website.

- Do you like their photographic style?
- Will you be able to work with their personality?
- Do you admire their work?
- How many photographers will be involved in your wedding?
- What is included in their package?
- How many hours will they be at your event?
- How much will they charge you for overtime?
- How long will it take to get the pictures back to you?
- How will your pictures be previewed? On their website or will they give you a CD?

Plan to have most of the classic pictures taken prior to your wedding ceremony saving only the poses of you and Mr. Wonderful together for after the ceremony. Taking the wedding party away from the festivities for an extended length of time to take pictures disappoints your guests who want to share this time with you. An experienced photographer will take their best pictures of your wedding in candid situations during the entire event. They will capture little nuances you neglected to notice at the time, but will find joy in the memories when you see them later on.

Plan to provide the photographer with a list of the traditional poses you would like taken as well as a list of the specific people, and combinations of people, you would like photographed such as family members, college friends, work friends, etc. Also, identify specific guests you would like them to catch in candid pictures. Introduce the photographer to the wedding coordinator or a special friend he can refer to if he has any questions or needs additional help.

If you do not think spending a lot of money on a photographer or videographer is the best use of your wedding dollars, ask several friends to bring their cameras and offer to pay for their pictures to be developed. Usually there is no cost for these pictures because everyone has digital cameras and they can email their pictures to you. You can post these snapshots on the Internet and share them with your guests and friends and family who were unable to attend the wedding.

Another way to involve your guests in your reception, and also have additional pictures, is to designate a picturesque background and ask a friend to take posed pictures of your guests. You can also leave disposable cameras at each table to encourage everyone to take their own pictures. In the process, they might take unusual pictures that may be more candid and intimate than those of your professional photographer. Their photographic participation will help them create their own experience and add to yours. It will also encourage people who might not get acquainted to introduce themselves. Request your friends walk around the tables and take pictures of small family groups and couples, as well as people they don't know. Your guests will have fun being in the pictures, as well as taking the pictures, and you will have a different visual record of your reception.

The memories created on your wedding day will be set in your mind forever. Photographs and a video will keep these special memories alive for you to visually enjoy and share with those friends and family who were unable to attend.

Videotaping your wedding captures the images of your wedding in a very different way and also preserves the audio portion of your wedding. A video is priceless because it allows you to hear and reminisce over the vows you spoke to each other and the speeches your loved ones delivered. If a videographer is not in your budget, rent a video camera and find a friend who will volunteer their services. If you think it is too big a responsibility for one person, ask your friends to get a team together and give each person the responsibility of videotaping a specific portion of the ceremony and reception. By spreading this task among several friends, you are not expecting one person to take on the full responsibility of making the video which would also limit their ability to participate as a guest. Involving several people in this project will increase your chances of having a very fun, interesting and complete video history of your special day! It will also narrow your chances of the entire video not turning out if one of the people assigned to the task didn't know what they were doing. Try to avoid this from happening by being certain they all have experience with a video camera.

FLOWERS
are the Thirteenth Most Important Detail

Flowers are one of the many areas where it is easy to overspend. Set a budget and decide what flowers are going to make the most dramatic statement. Arrange for the flowers at the ceremony to be transported to the reception by either the florist or several people with large vehicles. They can be used to decorate your reception area, banquet table and wedding cake cutting table.

Different kinds of flowers have different price tags. Keep in mind that you may be able to make the same statement with sweet peas as with roses. The location and time of year will also affect your floral decisions. Be flexible in your flower choices. If you use seasonal flowers, they will be more cost effective than exotic tulips or other varieties that have to be imported. You can also save money by using beautiful greenhouse plants displayed in baskets and embellished with a few cut flowers, ribbons or bows. Large vases containing unusual flowers displayed creatively can also add drama to your venue. If you want a grandiose floral look, think about renting trees in decorative containers.

Large elaborate bouquets may not always be the best choice for your tables because they may interfere with your guests' view and or conversations. One or or more flower arrangements creatively displayed on the tables and throughout your venue will be perfect to capture your style. You can also consider elevating your floral arrangements in vases designed specifically for your look and location. Indoors or outdoors, the focus will be on you, not the flowers, so don't go overboard.

Ways to Save the Dollars:
- Use flowers that are in season.
- Use flowers that are grown locally.
- Use a few dramatic flowers and fill in your arrangement with less expensive flowers and greenery.
- Choose a themed centerpiece that may or may not include flowers.
- Embellish a potted plant.
- Style an arrangement around a large candle.
- Float flowers and candles in a shallow bowl.
- Combine real flowers with artificial flowers.

PRE-WEDDING RECEPTION and/or REHEARSAL DINNER are the Fourteenth Most Important Details

Time, expense and logistics are the most significant deciding factors for having, or not having, a rehearsal dinner. You may think you have to have a rehearsal but you don't necessarily need to have a dinner afterwards. Especially if you don't have much time or some of your wedding participants live out of the area and cannot be at the wedding site prior to the wedding. If time is limited, the rehearsal can even be held the morning of the ceremony. In any event, it is very important to prepare a timeline for the wedding party and scripts for the people who have specific responsibilities. Most of the people in your wedding party will have been in several weddings so they will have a basic idea of what to do.

This is another example of why a wedding coordinator is valuable because they will be in attendance to manage everyone and tell them where they should be and when. At the ceremony, she will cue everyone and signal when they need to perform. The most important thing everyone needs to understand is they must be on time! With so many events going on in conjunction with the wedding weekend, it is easy for some people to become distracted.

Many people consider the rehearsal dinner a tradition and a private affair the night before the wedding. It is usually limited to one's immediate family and the wedding party. Others feel it is customary to invite out-of-town guests if they have traveled quite a distance. The problem is many times most of the guests are from out of town!

If you are having a destination wedding, you need to be prepared to take care of your guests because they have traveled a long way to celebrate with you. A big rehearsal dinner is comparable to doing two weddings in both cost and planning. It is a great way to get everyone together, but besides being expensive, it is exhausting and may affect everyone's energy and enthusiasm for the rest of the weekend. To avoid feeling obligated to entertain everyone who does not live locally, have the rehearsal and dinner on Thursday evening before most of the out-of-town guests arrive. Or, have the rehearsal earlier in the afternoon and forego the rehearsal dinner. Marsha tried to serve wine and snacks at her rehearsal but the wedding coordinator forbid her from serving any liquor. The wedding consultant wanted everyone's full attention on the rehearsal and she didn't want it to turn into a party!

From another perspective, a reception the night before the wedding is a nice way to greet your friends as they arrive. It gives your guests a designated place to go the first night they are in town and allows everyone the opportunity to get to know each other before the wedding. A pre-wedding reception is usually more casual, can be less expensive and is a great way for people to get acquainted or renew old friendships. Weddings also bring many people together who haven't met but come together with some commonality since they share a relationship with either you or Mr. Wonderful. A social function before the wedding offers the opportunity for people to connect and get organized for the events of the weekend.

Different locations offer different activities to keep your out-of-town guests occupied and entertained for the weekend. This does not mean you have to pay for their activities or be available as the hostess the entire weekend. You and Mr. Wonderful have chosen a great location so let them explore. However, it is considerate to provide some suggestions for entertainment and sightseeing before the wedding. The hotel concierge will provide you with information on what to do and where to go, and you can include this information on your Save-the-Date card, post it on your website and put it in the gift basket you will leave in their room. The local Chamber of Commerce and the Internet are always valuable resources for additional information about the area.

If you want to bring your out-of-town guests together before the wedding, but don't want to include them in the rehearsal dinner or host a pre-wedding reception because of your limited budget, you can:

- Provide guests with dinner suggestions at the hotel or in the area.
- Send small groups to local restaurants to get to know each other.
- Designate someone to arrange the evening and make reservations.
- Ask a friend who lives locally to host a wine and cheese party in your honor.
- Host a cocktail or desert reception later in the evening after the rehearsal dinner. This would be the least expensive and yet honor your guests who have traveled a long distance to witness and celebrate your marriage.

There are a number of opportunities to include other people in the preparation and responsibilities of your wedding day or wedding weekend. Give your friends and family the fun of getting involved. Assign them tasks or events such as golf, hikes, spa services, bus tours or anything

else you can find available in the area which does not involve your participation but will keep your guests occupied until the wedding ceremony. If
you want to make your guests feel like you are involved in their activities,
provide water bottles, golf hats, golf balls, or refreshments at each venue.
All of which can be chosen to reflect your wedding theme or personalized
with your wedding logo. Your guests will not expect you to be available
to them before the wedding and you aren't responsible for planning their
weekend. Remember, your wedding is the event everyone is there for!

Gift Baskets
Gift baskets for your out of town guests are a nice gesture.
There are hundreds of things you can find to put in a wedding gift
basket for your out of town guests such as wine, water, snacks, candles,
flashlights, bath oil, a list of available activities, bug spray, maps, a program for the weekend, contact numbers, etc. However, putting a gift
basket in everyone's room might be the first thing you eliminate if you
are running out of time or money. Also, this is a good job to assign to
someone who is creative at pulling everything together at the last minute.
It is difficult to assemble the baskets ahead of time and you may have too
many other things to do right before the wedding.

Wedding Breakfast
Serving a breakfast the morning after the wedding is not expected,
but it is appreciated, especially when you have a destination wedding
and almost all your guests are staying at the same location. This is usually
casual and the bride and groom are not expected to show up. But why
would you miss another time to celebrate when you have the rest of your
life together!

Other Parties
If your wedding brings a lot of people together, who might not see
each other very often, they may decide to plan their own social activity.

The planning and cost of these events should be the responsibility of the person organizing them. For example, if the groom's family and friends want to create an opportunity to spend more time together, they can host a separate, more personal event. Another example is if your wedding is in the wine country and some people want to go wine tasting, let them organize and pay for the transportation and wine tour themselves. You and Mr. Wonderful want to provide a memorable day for both you and your guests, but limit your responsibilities.

All of your planning has led to this moment so now just relax! You can't change anything. Accept that there is always a possibility that something may go wrong. Delegate different responsibilities to friends in advance and let them take care of the final details. Don't give your parents, children or bridesmaids any last minute assignments. They are almost as excited as you are! Focus on the moment and don't get focused on the details!

Stop every 15 minutes throughout the day or evening, take a breath and just look at what is going on around you. These will be your memories. The wedding goes by so fast and it will be over before you are ready to say goodbye to your guests.

HONEYMOON
is the Fifteenth Most Important Detail

Even though your marriage is at a certain time of year, it doesn't mean your wedding has to be immediately followed by your honeymoon. Due to work and family commitments, plus the fact that many out of town people came to celebrate your special day, you may want to delay your honeymoon plans. Also, depending on the location you choose, you may want to travel when the weather is the best or the crowds are smaller.

Honeymoons are intended to be a time when you can relax and be alone together after all the fun and joyous confusion of your wedding. Anytime after you marry you can consider all your vacations to be

---

Reception Quiz for Couples:

- What type of reception do you want?
- Where do you want your reception to be held?
- What kind of refreshments and/or food do you want to serve?
- How do you want the food served?
- Do want a Champagne toast?
- Do you want dancing at your reception?

❧

honeymoons. This one is just your launching pad! For couples marrying later in life, you may have children to consider. As we have mentioned throughout our book, it is important to include them in as much of the ceremony and building your new home together as possible. That is, everything except your honeymoon!

How and where you decide to celebrate your marriage after the ceremony will be up to you. You might be well traveled at this time of your life but sharing a new adventure together will be a wonderful way to start your marriage. Relax and let your groom create the honeymoon of this dreams!

Many later in life couples have accumulated more than enough household goods and are electing to register for their honeymoon instead of requesting traditional gifts. Everyone likes to give a wedding gift, they want it to be well received and something the couple will remember them by. Who wouldn't remember you helped support their honeymoon? Cruise lines, resorts, hotels and other destination points offer these services.

Honeymoon Registries

There are many registry sites just for the purpose of planning a honeymoon. But going to a specific honeymoon registration site is easier and provides more specific information to help you customize your

---

Honeymoon Quiz for Couples:

- Where do you each want to go?
- Do you want a beach holiday or cultural city tour?
- Do you want a mountain adventure or exotic safari?
- Do you want a cruise or an all-inclusive resort?
- How long do you want to be away?
- What time of year do you want to travel?

---

honeymoon travel plans. There are several well-known honeymoon travel registries: thebigday.com, sendusoff.com, honeymoonwishes.com, travelersjoy.com and wandersble.com.

The first task is to plan your complete travel itinerary. After that, the registry will divide your trip into affordable components so family and friends can make their gift specific to an item on your itinerary. These items could include a one night's stay, cultural trip through a city, lunches and dinners at well known restaurants, a sunset boat cruise, as well as sports activities such as golf, tennis, scuba diving, fishing and so forth.

The best time of year to travel depends on where you want to go and there are travel bargains everywhere if you have the time to research them. If you want to travel to a distant location for what you hope to be one of the most memorable trips of your life, you may not want to sacrifice when and where you want to go in order to get a discounted price. It is also unlikely the plans for your honeymoon will coincide with the most inexpensive time there is to travel. Use the Internet to research where you want to go and focus on the weather. Also, be aware of the important holidays celebrated during that time because it is very inconvenient to arrive at unfamiliar place only to find everything is closed because of a holiday.

And don't forget travel insurance!

Cruises

All-inclusive cruise packages are very cost effective way to get the most for your money. It makes it easier to budget because your room, food, entertainment and transportation are included and you don't have to worry about tipping or extras unless specified in the contract.

Some discount cruise line websites are CuiseDeals.com, CruiseOnly.com and VacationsToGo.com.

All-Inclusive Resorts

Like cruises, these all-inclusive resorts where after you arrive, and plop down your suitcase, you are there to stay! There is no unpacking and re-packing each and you and Mr. Wonderful can relax and take advantage of their many activities…or not! Some discount Resort websites are Sandals.com, Occidentalhotels.com, Superclubs.com. AllinclusiveOutlet.com and ClassicVacations.com. Many of the vacation packages these resorts offer are in the Caribbean, Hawaii and Mexico.

Most of us know the usual travel websites for the best rates on airfare, lodging and car rentals. However, for finding great rates on four and five star properties around the world, we have found AllLuxuryhotels.com, LastMinuteTravel.com and QuikBook.com. are good resources and Last Minute Travel and Quik Book are better for spur of the moment decisions.

Beach Resorts

Some of the most romantic honeymoon locations are found on beaches and most of them offer honeymoon packages. Do your Internet research by deciding where you want to go, and the best time of the year to go there, then evaluate the resorts that are available. You don't want to be blown off the sand and have an unexpected hurricane ruin your plans.

Other Honeymoon Venues

There are many other honeymoon destinations besides the beach. Europe, Asia and Africa deserve their own book. However, if you don't want to leave the country, most resorts have great packages that provide a lot of activities for all seasons. But who cares about activities when you are on your honeymoon?

Now that you are married, have planned your honeymoon and are relishing in the glow of happiness and ecstasy, we will leave you with one thought;

The most wonderful of all things in life is the discovery of another human being with whom one's relationship has a growing depth, beauty and joy as the years increase. This inner progressiveness of love between two human beings is a most marvelous thing; it cannot be found by looking for it or by passionately wishing for it. It is sort of a divine accident, and the most wonderful of all things in life.

-Hugh Walpole, writer

Details Notes:

CHAPTER FIVE

MLL WEDDING PLANNER

Timeline

AND QUIZZES

Timeline

Ideally, plan for everything to take 25% more time than you expected! Time management will reduce some anxiety but expect some natural jitters and turn them into excitement and anticipation!

The best way to begin planning your wedding is to establish a timeline that itemizes every element you can identify that is necessary to create your celebration. It is helpful if it is designed so you can check things off as you work through each decision or detail, starting with the location and ending with your honeymoon. It is difficult to identify all the decisions that have to be made and your list will expand as you work through the details involved in each element. Also, keep project completion dates and detailed notes. It is critical you make decisions that are both reasonable for you, your finances and time frame. And make it your goal to plan a wedding that works comfortably within those limits.

At times you may feel overwhelmed with all the preparations. We certainly did! Hopefully you will have the luxury of several months to plan and manage the items on your list without feeling besieged with details.

Throughout all the planning and implementation it is important to occasionally stop, breathe and remember to enjoy the fun and excitement of the process. This is your dream come true!

We can't impress on you enough how important it is, in fact, how crucial it is to give yourself lots of time. Everything takes more time than you think. You are naturally busy with your everyday life and we understand that you never seem to have any extra time as it is.

As a modern mature bride getting married later in life, you think you can handle any stressful situation. However, the excitement and added pressure of getting married brings a completely new dimension to the definition of the word…stress!

THE IDEAL TIMELINE

We have based our timeline on a year, but if you are marrying sooner, it will still work for you – JUST FASTER!

Six to Twelve Months before
- Decide on the location for your wedding and reception. Now book it!
- Decide on the date for your wedding.
- Decide on your wedding party.
- Decide on your wedding style (elegant, formal, casual, informal).
- Announce your engagement to family and friends.
- Arrange for your family and friends to meet each other if they haven't already.
- Hire a wedding consultant if you think you need one.
- Create a website for family & friends to follow your celebration plans.
- Discuss your budget and priorities.
- Start looking at bridal magazines and blogs to help you identify the style you would like for your wedding dress.
- Compile a guest list.
- Shop for a wedding dress.
- Shop for your attendants' dresses.
- Go to Bridal Shows and Fairs.
- Research and hire venders.
- Book the rehearsal dinner location or any other pre-post wedding events.
- Research stationery options.
- Get in Shape – NOW!

Six Months
- Buy your wedding dress.
- Shop for accessories: headpiece, shoes, veil, etc.
- Decide on your attendants' dresses.
- Decide on who will Officiate.
- Decide on your stationery.
- Send save the date cards.

- Review your exercise program and get a trainer if your efforts are not showing results.
- Book transportation and hotel rooms.
- Plan your honeymoon.
- Create a finalized guest list. Review the addresses and contact information.
- Compile a list of your vendors and wedding party contacts.
- Update your website.
- Set up a bridal registry if needed.

Four to Six Months before
- Confirm all arrangements already under contract.
- Continue reviewing and selecting your stationery.
- Reserve all linens and party rentals.
- Order wedding favors for your guests and attendants.
- Shop for your wedding rings.
- Finalize your honeymoon plans.

Two to Four Months before
- Identify who is going to Officiate your wedding.
- Select the perfect wedding cake.
- Meet with the caterer and review the menus, wine list, servers, etc.
- Review and select your wedding vows and music.
- Research marriage license requirements, especially if it is a destination wedding.
- If traveling overseas for your wedding or honeymoon, make certain your passports are up-to-date.

Four to Eight Weeks before
- Obtain your wedding license from your city's County Clerk.
- Order tuxedos for the groom and attendants.
- Mail invitations 6 to 8 weeks before your wedding date.
- Have a method of recording the RSVP's and meal selections.
- Confirm dates, deposits and details with your vendors.
- Consider taking a dancing lesson with Mr. Wonderful.
- Confirm details with your attendants.
- Continue to write thank you notes, when needed.

Three to Five Weeks before
- Do a "hair and make-up trial."
- Schedule your final dress fitting with all the appropriate undergarments and shoes.
- Send out rehearsal dinner invitations.
- Complete name change documents where applicable.
- Pick up wedding rings and check the engraving.
- Buy gifts for your attendants.
- Purchase your guest book, toasting flutes, cake servers, unity candle and other necessities.

Finalize and confirm:
- Shot list with your photographer
- Song list with musicians for ceremony, cocktail reception, dinner and dancing
- Timeline for the reception and who is giving the toasts
- Wedding night and honeymoon plans.
- Follow up with guests you haven't heard from yet.
- Create seating arrangements for the rehearsal dinner and reception.

One to Two Weeks before
- Assign a friend to be in charge of taking your toasting glasses, cake knife and any other personal items to the reception to give to the caterer.
- Give the caterer and venue the final guest count.
- Review seating arrangements and place cards.
- Write your rehearsal dinner toast.
- Confirm arrival times and finalize the timeline with family members, wedding party and venders.
- Put together your "Marrying Later in Life" emergency bridal kit.
- Schedule your final beauty treatments: manicure, facial, massage, waxing, brow shaping, etc.
- Check the weather report to see if you need to make alternate plans.
- Start packing for your honeymoon!
- Pick up your gown. Beautiful!
- If you are traditional, look for something old, new, borrowed and blue.

The Day Before

Assign friends or family the following tasks:

- Double check that all your wedding day items are packed and ready to go.
- Don't forget the rings and the marriage license!
- Review the final payments to vendors and put them in clearly marked envelopes.
- Ask someone to be responsible for taking your gifts and belongings home after the reception, including the top tier of your wedding cake.
- Confirm who is going to return the tuxedos and any other rentals from the day.
- Have a manicure and pedicure to relax.
- Get ready for the rehearsal.
- Get a good night sleep!

Your Wedding Day

- Relax and remain calm.
- Allow plenty of time to get ready.
- Remember to eat something, especially protein.
- Keep yourself hydrated.
- Take a deep breath and make the most of your special day!
- Be certain to personally thank everyone for coming and celebrating your day with you.

After the Honeymoon

- Write thank you notes.
- Complete your registry and return any duplicate or unwanted gifts.
- Have your wedding dress cleaned.
- Contact your photographer/videographer.

Timeline Notes:

CHAPTER SIX

AND QUIZZES

The Kit

Love the man who you have made your husband every day from this day forward!

We recommend you create a special kit with all the basic essentials for wedding day emergencies. It is always better to be prepared because there are bound to be some unexpected situation that arises during your wedding event. The items you choose for your "Emergency Bridal Kit" should prepare you to solve an array of problems including items for dental care, manicure repairs and potential dress disasters.

There are many creative solutions for the container you will need to organize the "emergency" items you want to have with you at your wedding. A fishing tackle box with separate drawers including a big space on the bottom makes a great container for small and large items. Or, if you want something more feminine, a large hanging cosmetic or lingerie bag works beautifully well. They are especially useful when they are designed with clear plastic pockets. An "all in one" hanging bag will travel easier along with your dress and accessories. You can then store your individual items in Ziploc bags, so you can find and get to things easier.

A more masculine "Dopp" bag would be a very thoughtful and practical gift for Mr. Wonderful. Fill it with the obvious things you think he will need, and then let him add his own favorites. He might think of things for both of you that hadn't been included on your list!

You may have had some traveling experiences during your courtship and have established some patterns or habits for who is responsible for different situations. However, packing for this occasion might open up some new areas for discussion.

Will your fiancé expect you to remember "all the toiletries" or will you each pack for your individual needs? Don't assume – ask. Your Mr. W. may have expectations you are not aware of. Some men assume their wives will take care of the "details" in life which may include packing.

You want Mr. Wonderful to feel special, and you want to anticipate his needs but packing is a very personal and individual process. In your future together, he may assume it is your responsibility to take care of all of his needs not only at home but also when traveling. You should know this role ahead of time.

If you do not think this is your role then it will lead to an interesting discussion. One of many!

After you have assembled the items you think should be included in your Emergency Bridal Kit, introduce the kit to your bridal party and suggest they get involved in contributing items they think you may have forgotten.

"Assembling an Emergency Bridal Kit" would be a great theme for a bridal shower! Or requesting individual items would be a great gift suggestion if you are having a bachelorette event.

Be sure to assign one of your attendants to be responsible for your Emergency Bridal Kit during the wedding day and refer to her if there are any incidents that involve emergency or "last minute" attention.

The Bride's Kit:
- Asthma inhaler or other medication
- Aspirin or other pain reliever
- Antacids
- Baby Wipes (for stains)
- Band aids (clear)
- Bobby, barrettes or hair pins
- Bottled water
- Breath mints
- Chalk or ivory-colored soap to cover dress stains or lipstick stains on the groom's shirt collar
- Comb & Brush
- Crochet hook to get at button holes

- Curling Iron
- Double-sided tape for quick hem fixes
- Emery board
- Earring backs (extra)
- Feminine emergency items
- Hair spray
- Hair Dryer
- Hand cream
- Kleenex
- Lip gloss
- Makeup!
- Mirror
- Moisturizer
- Nail polish and remover
- Nail File
- Nail Glue
- Oil absorbing facial wipes
- Q tips
- Rubber bands
- Safety pins in assorted sizes; straight pins
- Scissors
- Sewing kit with thread to match the colors of the bride's and bridesmaid's dresses plus black
- Small sewing kit with scissors
- Small steamer (only if the bride or someone already owns one and wants to bother tucking it in the bag)
- Stain remover pads
- Static-cling spray
- Straws for a drink without messing up lipstick
- Stockings (at least 2 pairs)
- Superglue for a broken heel

- Talcum powder also works on liquid stains especially if the spill contains grease
- Tampons (if still needed!)
- The Bride's (color) nail polish
- Toothbrush & Toothpaste
- Touch-up cosmetics
- Tweezers
- Two sided fabric tape to keep straps in place
- White-out for emergencies not handled by chalk
- Wrinkle spray

The items in your "Emergency Bridal Kit" should take care of everything from a nervous stomach, a stain on your dress, an emergency skin blemish, food caught in your teeth, an unexpected rip in your attendant's hem down to a big pin to fix your bustle if it doesn't hang correctly.

The Groom's Kit:
- Aspirin or Pain reliever
- Band Aids-clear
- Bottled Water
- Comb & Brush
- Emery Board
- Hand Cream
- Handkerchief
- Q tips
- Razor
- Small sewing kit with scissors
- Talcum Powder
- Toothbrush & Toothpaste
- Q-tips
- Snacks
- H2O

Also, tuck in a special message for him to read and think about you when you are both getting dressed.

If you really want to be prepared, you might consider the following items. However, I don't think they will all fit in your Bridal Kit container!

Miscellaneous Items:
- Backup ceremony music on CD
- Duct tape
- Fishing line
- Hammer
- Lighter or matches
- Small glue gun
- Small step ladder
- Toothpicks
- Wire
- Press & Seal

A replica of your Bridal Kit also makes a wonderful gift to pass on to another friend marrying later in life and not knowing where to start!

It is our desire that by reading *Marrying Later in Life* you will give yourself permission to make your wedding the one you have always imagined. The day you dreamed about when you were trying on your 6th bridesmaid dress and your mother said it was "very special" to be asked to participate in your second cousin's wedding; the day you wished for when you were the maid of honor for your little sister; the day you hoped for after you had been divorced for six months; the day when you were trying to understand how to re-enter the dating world; or the day your ex-husband remarried.

Now all of that is behind you. It is your turn to be the bride and enjoy the day that will become one of the most memorable occasions of your life!

From this day forward,
You shall not walk alone.
My heart will be your shelter,
And my arms will be your home.

The Kit Notes:

About The Authors

For over 30 years, Elizabeth and Marsha have built successful business careers in the areas of food styling and medical billing.

Then, 12 years ago, the ladies found themselves in a wonderful yet confusing time of planning and orchestrating a wedding appropriate for their age and family circumstances. However, all their personal and business experience did not prepare them for the decisions they had to make getting married at this time of their life and planning a wedding as a mature bride. It was then they realized that no one in the wedding industry was addressing brides in their age category. As a growing number of Internet and dating sites became available and more and more couples over 40 were getting married, there still were no resources for women in these circumstances. So the girls decided to write one themselves.

In the process of scripting this book, it became obvious to Elizabeth and Marsha that *Marrying Later in Life* had to deal with more than just wedding plans for the modern mature bride. There were also many more difficult decisions that were not pertinent to the younger bride. So, they designed *Marrying Later in Life* to fill the hole in the donut.

How Elizabeth and Marsha Met

Sometime in the late 90's Elizabeth and Marsha met in a yoga class through the introduction of a man they both had dated but with whom neither of them had remained involved. It turned out he wasn't the first man they both had dated. They found out they had dated three of the same men in the same town! They decided these men must all have had a "thing" for short blondes! Over the years and during many early morning walks (which is great therapy second only to shopping), Elizabeth and Marsha shared both their professional and personal lives. They became close friends, understanding and experiencing each other's joys and sorrows.

Elizabeth found her Mr. Wonderful first, but that had no effect on their friendship as it continued to grow. Five years later, Marsha met Mike, her Mr. Wonderful, and looked to Elizabeth for advice on how to plan a wedding as a bride who was older than most. Elizabeth knew after her divorce that if she remarried she would want a traditional wedding. So her wedding decisions were tailored to that style. Marsha's first wedding was a formal church ceremony, which was great but didn't seem to be compatible with her vision for her second marriage. She wanted a wedding that focused more on her new life and the family that she and Mike were creating with their second marriage. She didn't know how or where to start making wedding plans but she did know that she wanted a beautiful, sensitive ceremony in a memorable place. And most of all, she wanted to include her new blended family and close friends. Finding a beautiful dress that was appropriate for the location and considering the time of year and her age was a definite must. But how do you plan a wedding when you are an older bride was the question nagging at the back of her mind. It was on one of their walks that she asked Elizabeth this question and it was this question that became the catalyst for "Marrying Later in Life".

But we digress; Marsha was having a difficult time trying to figure out the appropriate style for her wedding. She knew she wanted her wedding to reflect the love, fun and friendship she and Mike shared. It also needed to be tasteful for their age, comfortable, meaningful, beautiful, and above all respectful of the new adult blended family they were creating with their marriage. It was at this time she made a comment to Elizabeth about writing a book that would help women who were going through the same challenges of planning a wedding later in their life. Thus, she began forging ahead in her usual energized fashion and created a beautiful destination wedding that everyone loved!

After Marsha's wedding, Elizabeth asked if she was going to write "that book" which she had mentioned on one of their walks. Marsha had initially forgotten about her comment, but with Elizabeth's encouragement, they decided they should put their thoughts together in writing. That was like Oprah's "Ah Ha" moment and the genesis of this collaboration.

To get started, Marsha and Elizabeth decided to spend one afternoon a week putting their thoughts down in writing. They hoped to eventually collate their notes into a book but they kept getting sidetracked with everyday commitments, designing a website and all sorts of other distractions. Years passed, the economy for publishing books changed, but their focus was always the same – let's finish our book! It got so they didn't want anyone to know they were still working on the project since they had been writing it for so long. But as the years passed, the acceptance of Internet dating became the norm and more and more people were getting married later in life. Still, when Elizabeth and Marsha researched the bookstores and the Internet, there weren't many books or even articles on the topic of later in life dating, marriages or weddings. It became apparent that this was still a subject where some women might need guidance so they decided to focus on completing their book. Getting married later in life had become an even more relevant issue than when they had first started writing about it. And, it was the perfect time to bring more attention to the issues, challenges and joys that come with planning a wedding as a mature bride.

Elizabeth's Story

My first wedding ceremony was hardly traditional! It was in the early 70's and my fiancé and I were typical products of the hippie generation. Since I was from the East Coast and my husband-to-be was from

California, the festivities began with grand bicoastal parties at both parents' homes. Following those events, we had a lovely wedding at my
husband's family residence. The actual ceremony was small and intimate
with only 60 guests. I recall being unable to walk down the aisle. Actually,
when I reminisce about it now, I can't remember if there even was an
aisle. I just remember that I was told to appear from behind one of the
bedroom doors and walk into the living room where the wedding would
take place. It was a casual affair to be sure. But before the main event, I
vividly remember lying on my sister-in-law's bed frightened half to death
at the thought of being in front of all those people who were actually
my close friends and family, and saying my marriage vows. However, my
fears actually ran much deeper. I remember wondering if I really wanted
to get married. Was I ready? Was he the right man for me? Maybe I
should have listened to my first frightened instincts when I broke down
crying while picking out my china and sterling. Everything just became
overwhelming. I felt someone else should be getting married but me. A
wedding is supposed to be a joyous and happy time but that wasn't how
I felt. However, I went along with the festivities because I was afraid to
disappoint everyone, especially my family and soon-to-be in laws.

As I lay on the bed full of apprehension and anxiety, my fiancé was
leaning over me trying to comfort and reassure me there was nothing
to worry about. It didn't help much. Little did I know that my instincts
were correct; I was divorced three years later. In fact, the divorce was
settled on the anniversary of my wedding day, at which time I decided
that my next wedding, if there ever were to be one, would certainly be
different. Very different!

During the next 20 years, my days were filled with many dates, boy-
friends, and returned engagement rings. My friends would always ask
why I wasn't interested in a particular man they thought was wonderful.
They would say, "What's wrong with him?" and I would respond without
much enthusiasm "He's great but . . ." The word "but" is a significant
relationship stopper. At least it was for me. There would be no "buts"

when I married again! So, when I finally met the man I knew I would spend the rest of my life with, it was very different. Right from the beginning there were no doubts with Steve. There were no questions: no ifs, ands, or buts. It was magical from the first date, and in time it became a wonderful reality.

Steve and I were raised with similar backgrounds and held close to our hearts the same mid-western values. Even though our paths in life were quite different and our careers were miles apart, Steve specialized in intervention cardiology and I was a food stylist involved in advertising and commercial film production, we were perfect for each other.

After my first marriage ended without children, I thought I would never have the opportunity to raise a family. But to my surprise, I met Steve who had been married for 23 years and had three grown children. Although they came into my life as young adults, I was thrilled to welcome them into my world. Steve's 25-year-old son, Peter, continued to live in our home for 6 years after our wedding. Not experiencing children of my own, this presented a challenge. Peter is a very nice young man, and what others would have considered a problem or inconvenience, I approached as a learning experience. I learned to be a friend and confidante rather than try to act as his mother. Most importantly, I felt welcomed by all of Steve's family and we started to bond immediately.

Steve and I chose to be married in my family's hometown in Ohio. However, living in Southern California, while planning a wedding around aging parents with traditional wedding ideas, was a challenge. For my second wedding, I did not want to have the same experience as my first wedding. And although I was no longer 23, I still wanted to walk down the aisle wearing a long dress with a bustle and a veil. I wanted to be given away by my father and formally commit myself to the man with whom I was going to spend the rest of my life. Although I didn't wear white, I did have a flowing gown and relished in all the wedding traditions including the first dance with my husband. It was magical.

Marsha's Story

I fell in love with my first husband, Tom, at 17 and we married as soon as we graduated from college. Tom wanted to be a physician so we moved several times for his medical training and military obligations. We finally ended up in Southern California where we raised two children and had a great marriage – until we didn't. At which time I found myself 46, single, alone and with two sons still in college.

After being married 24 years, I found being divorced confusing. For years I had been focused on building a life with my husband, supporting his medical career and raising our two sons. It was a long road to the end of this marriage and I was disappointed and emotionally exhausted. It was also a time in which I had to make some big decisions about what I was going to do about my finances and what direction I wanted to focus my energy. Since my boys were at school, I was fortunate to have the personal freedom to plan my daily life around myself. It offered me a new perspective that I had never known before.

I had been working to provide a service to the local physician community but it became obvious I had to figure out how to support myself with the small, medical billing company I had started. My circumstances made it easy to focus and turn my energy into the challenge of learning how to build a business. I was fortunate to have been at the right place, at the right time and have the opportunity to work with wonderful people. After the divorce, working was the easy part. My day was defined, filled with challenges and a lot of social interaction but this "busyness" also helped me disguise that I wasn't doing much to improve my social life. Finally, one of my old male college friends took me to dinner with the intention of telling me I had to learn how to date.

I was stunned to realize dating was a skill and someone I respected was telling me I didn't know how to date or wasn't very good at it. He suggested I try a new matchmaking concept that his friends were starting which turned out to be a precursor to eHarmony and Match.com. It was called "Just for Coffee." It involved a small membership fee which entitled you to be introduced to other men/women in your community. The introductions were by telephone (pre-Internet!), and after the initial introduction, you were left to your own discretion if you wanted to meet in person - the rest was up to you. Coincidentally, Elizabeth had also been introduced to "Just for Coffee" and that is how we ended up dating some of the same men! Since we live in a very large community, it is amazing how many times our lives crossed before we finally met.

The dating service turned out to be just what I needed to get me actively interested in my social life. However, there was always a "but" with each candidate, which meant I had to work on my attitude and expectations. It was also an indication that I wasn't ready to have a serious relationship. The timing wasn't right or the gentleman wasn't right.

Then Mike came into my life. I found him rather magically in the office next to mine. After years of running my own company, I realized I had too many balls in the air and needed a CEO to add the discipline and expertise to take my company to the next level. I eventually found Mike and he agreed to take over the reins of the company. At first I didn't know if I even liked him because now a man was telling me how to run my own company. To be fair, he really didn't enjoy becoming the CEO of a company with the founder in the office next door who had opinions. However, we did respect each other for what we individually brought to the business.

I thought I was happy. I always had fun, male companionship in my life and the years went by until "out of the blue" Mike asked me for a date. I was shocked, but curious, so I accepted. The happy ending to my story is that after a few years of dating and getting to know each other on a personal level, we were married.

We had a fabulous, beautiful, memorable wedding that fulfilled all my dreams. However, in the beginning of the process, I was completely confused. I didn't know where to start. I didn't know what style was appropriate for a bride at my age and I couldn't find any resources to guide me. My situation was different from Elizabeth's. My parents were deceased and my sister and two sons were my only family. Mike has two daughters so bringing our families together was very important. All of our adult children were cooperative in their interest to get to know each other, and to our continued delight, they have become best friends. Their family backgrounds are very similar and outside activities and intellectual interests are very much the same. Mike and I now have a very fun, much bigger family that keeps growing with weddings and grandbabies. And because our children are so important to us, we chose to plan our wedding around our new blended family and limited our guest list to relatives and close friends.

❧

Elizabeth and Marsha sincerely hope you have enjoyed reading their book as much as they enjoyed writing it!

PS: After reading *Marrying Later in Life*, you may have additional questions and suggestions. We encourage you to contact Elizabeth and Marsha on their website and interact with their blog and venders. www.MarryingLaterinLife.com.

Acknowledgments

We wish to express our gratitude to some very special people who helped us along the way: Sherry Price, Suzie Janeski, Gia Lucy, Jessica Prentice, Robin Swift, Leann Baggetta, and Charles and Tracy Wilson.

Made in the USA
San Bernardino, CA
03 November 2013